YOUR CHILD CAN SUCCEED IN SCHOOL

100 Common-Sense Answers to Frequently Asked Questions

by Dorothy Rubin, Ph.D.

THE COLLEGE OF NEW JERSEY

Fearon Teacher Aids
A Division of Frank Schaffer Publications, Inc.

Editorial Director: Kristin Eclov
Copy Editor: Lisa Schwimmer Marier
Cover and Interior Design: RedLane Studio

Fearon Teacher Aids products were formerly manufactured and distributed by American Teaching Aids, Inc., a subsidiary of Silver Burdett Ginn, and are now manufactured and distributed by Frank Schaffer Publications, Inc. FEARON, FEARON TEACHER AIDS, and the FEARON balloon logo are marks used under license from Simon & Schuster, Inc.

Fearon Teacher Aids
A Division of Frank Schaffer Publications, Inc.
23740 Hawthorne Boulevard
Torrance, CA 90505-5927

FE211001

Table of Contents

Introduction 7

24. What kinds of books should I read aloud to my preschooler?

25. Is it normal for a child to want the same book read over and over again?

26. What kinds of questions should I ask my child about the story that I am reading aloud?

27. When is a child ready for kindergarten?

28. What is the "School Entry Questionnaire"?

29. Why do some parents choose to keep children out of kindergarten an extra year?

30. What are the states' entry dates for kindergarten?

31. What is the difference between "reading readiness" and "emergent literacy"?

32. What has led the television industry to provide ratings for their shows?

33. What effect, if any, does violence in fairy tales have on young children?

34. When should children learn to read?

35. What is the definition of reading?

36. What is a balanced reading program?

37. Is it possible for children to understand something when it is read aloud but not when they are reading it themselves?

38. What is word recognition?

39. What are some word recognition strategies?

40. Why do some children lack word recognition skills?

41. How can parents determine if children are "really" reading?

42. What are some educational reasons for children *not* learning to read in first grade?

43. What is the role of children reading aloud?

44. Is oral reading more important than silent reading?

45. What can be done to help children in the early grades gain the skills they need to become effective readers?

46. What can parents do to have input in the school's reading program?

47. What is the place of phonics in a school's reading program?

48. What kinds of phonics skills should children be learning in school?

49. What kinds of comprehension skills should children be learning in school?

50. What is the relationship of vocabulary to reading?

51. What should be done for a child who learned to read before kindergarten?

52. Why do some children from good home backgrounds *not* learn how to read?

53. What is the relationship of reading to school dropouts?

54. Who are the majority of school dropouts?

55. Will an army of volunteers help children become good readers?

83. What kind of sex information should be given to young children?

84. What are some questions that schools should be prepared to answer concerning their family-life program for young children?

85. What can schools do to help parents talk to their children about sex?

86. How important is the first-grade teacher?

87. Should children be retained in school?

88. What should be done for a child who has been retained a grade level?

89. Is learning in a single-gender environment better?

90. What are some noneducative gender differences?

91. What are some educative gender differences?

92. What is the purpose of within-class ability grouping?

93. What should parents know about the sequence of writing skills in children?

94. Why are some schools mandating uniforms for their students?

95. What is the role of teachers in helping children fit in socially in class?

96. What can be done to make parent-teacher conferences effective for both parents and teachers?

97. When should parent-teacher conferences take place?

98. Should young children receive an allowance?

99. How do you define allowance for children?

100. What should parents of young children know about allowance?

Introduction

Have you ever wondered whether you were doing the right things to help your child?
Have you ever wondered whether to send your child to preschool?
Have you ever wanted to know more about your child's reading program?

Relax. *Your Child Can Succeed in School* answers all these questions, as well as many more. Most parents want to do the best they possibly can for their children. The problem is, many parents don't know what to do. This book gives you the information you need to help your child succeed in school. Dr. Dorothy Rubin is a newspaper columnist, author, and well-known educator. *Your Child Can Succeed in School* is based on questions and letters Dr. Rubin has received from parents just like you.

This excellent collection is founded on sound psychological principles, avoids educational jargon, and takes nothing for granted. In addition, this book is organized into general categories using a question and answer format, so busy parents can quickly pick and choose those questions they would like answered.

An Early Childhood Parent and Child Activities section is also included to provide interested parents with enjoyable educational activities that are precursors for reading and subsequent success in school.

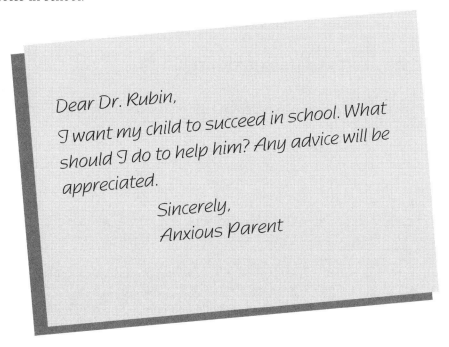

Dear Dr. Rubin,
I want my child to succeed in school. What should I do to help him? Any advice will be appreciated.
Sincerely,
Anxious Parent

Dear Anxious Parent,

Don't be so anxious. Your anxiety can transfer to your child. The fact that you are an interested and concerned parent is commendable and an important first step in helping your child. My book, *Your Child Can Succeed in School,* has lots of answers to help you.

Sincerely yours,

Dr. Dorothy Rubin

Dr. Dorothy Rubin

100 Q & As Parents: Children's First Teachers

Question 1: Why are parents considered children's first teachers?

Dear Dr. Rubin,

In my school district, parents are not encouraged to visit the schools. Don't all school personnel know that parents are children's first teachers? Perhaps if you write about this point, I could bring in your reply to the principal of my children's school.

> Sincerely,
> Frustrated Parent

Dear Frustrated Parent,

Many young children are curious about words and the world around them, and those they go to for help are the obvious ones—their parents. Yes, parents are children's first teachers. Hardly anyone would question a parent's right to help his or her child learn. For example, how many times have parents been involved in similar dialogues with their children?

> *"Daddy, what does the sign say?"*
> > "It says, 'STOP.'"

> *"Mommy, what is this word on the cereal box?"*
> > "The word is 'good.'"

And so it goes.
Obviously, parents are children's first teachers.

Question 2: What is the "Parent Report Card"?

Dear Dr. Rubin,

Thank you for sending me the Parent Report Card. I filled it out and was shocked to find that I came up short in areas I shouldn't have. Please help me. I know that I am doing many things right. I love my children and want to do the best for them. What do you suggest?

Sincerely,
Concerned Parent

P.S. Please send me another copy of the Parent Report Card, so I can fill it out again in a few months.

Dear Concerned Parent,

You have moved a giant step forward. Now that you realize you need some help and are interested in obtaining that help, you are on the road to becoming a better parent. This is very positive. I suggest that you check your Parent Report Card. Choose an area that you want to improve and follow these easy steps.

1. Choose the topic and questions from this book that deal with the area you want to improve.

2. Read the material.

3. Practice the ideas.

4. Continue practicing the ideas!

GOOD LUCK!

NOTES

Date _____   Parent's Name _____

Child's Name _____

THE PARENT REPORT CARD

Specific Ratings	Satisfactory	Needs Improvement	Unsatisfactory
1. I listen to my child.			
2. I read aloud to my child.			
3. I discuss things with my child.			
4. I spend time with my child.			
5. I ask my child good questions.			
6. I help my child.			
7. I encourage my child.			
8. I am patient.			
9. I take my child to interesting places.			
General Ratings	**Satisfactory**	**Needs Improvement**	**Unsatisfactory**
Child/parent relationship			
Teacher/parent relationship			
Desire to help child			

NOTES

Question 3: What is the difference between "quality time" and "reality time"?

Dear Dr. Rubin,

You recently wrote about "reality time" in your newspaper column. What are you talking about? Is this just another way of saying "quality time"?

Sincerely,
Curious Parent

Dear Curious Parent,

No, "reality time" is different from "quality time." "Quality time" requires making a value judgment. Also, I do not like to talk about "quality time" in relation to children and especially young children. "Reality time" is the actual time you spend with your child. This could happen while you are making a bed together, cooking or baking together, going for a walk, reading a story together, or just spending some quiet time together.

Every moment you spend with your child does not have to be filled with "pearls of wisdom." Think about it—if your child perceives that the only time you spend together is related to your trying to teach him or her something, your child may begin to react negatively to you and to school.

Question 4: What kinds of roles have parents played in school?

Dear Dr. Rubin,

What kinds of roles have parents played in their children's schools? I remember when I went to school, my parents hardly ever visited my school. They felt that if they were asked to go to school, there was something wrong. Also, at that time, teachers seemed to have the attitude of "hands off" when it came to school work.

Things seem to have changed a lot. Is this my imagination or what?

Sincerely,
Inquisitive Parent

Dear Inquisitive Parent,

Actually, parental involvement in the schools is not a new phenomenon. Parents sit on Boards of Education, they are involved in parent-teacher associations, parent councils, parent clubs, and other school-related programs. Parents help formulate school policy, have a say in curriculum matters, and even help to choose textbooks. Parents definitely have a voice in school matters. However, until recently, parents have not been encouraged to take an active role in working with their own children, particularly in the area of reading.

Years ago, teaching was considered the sole domain of the educator, and believe it or not, parents who wanted to teach their children were often looked upon as meddlers, troublemakers, and outsiders. At best they were looked upon as well-meaning but unknowledgeable, and until the late 1950s, they were admonished not to teach their children to read at home.

Today, in school districts across the country, parents, as well as grandparents, are looked upon as partners in their children's learning and potential resources rather than unknowing meddlers. This is as it should be.

So, the answer to your query is that, yes, things have changed a lot, but we still have a long way to go. The amount of parental involvement is directly related to the individual school and the school principal. Principals who have a warm, inviting atmosphere in their schools and encourage parental visits and involvement will obviously get more parental input than those who mouth the proper words but in reality, try to keep parents at arm's length.

NOTES

100 Q&As *Understanding Our Children*

Question 5: **How is intelligence defined?**

Dear Dr. Rubin,

The other night, my friends and I were discussing the concept of intelligence. We all defined it differently. Please help straighten us out.

> Sincerely,
> Grateful Parent

Dear Grateful Parent,

You chose quite a topic to discuss. Usually, when the topic of intelligence is brought up, the atmosphere becomes highly charged. Hardly anyone seems to regard this topic objectively.

Many definitions of intelligence exist, but the one most often used is that intelligence refers to the ability to do abstract reasoning. Intelligence is something that cannot be directly observed or directly measured.

Some psychologists define intelligence as problem-solving ability based on a hierarchical organization of two things—symbolic representations and strategies for processing information.

From the latter definition, we can see that those of us who have good strategies for processing information—that is, we know what goes together and what does not—will do better than those who are not good at categorizing information. Some psychologists still use a definition that was coined in the early twentieth century which states that "intelligence is what the intelligence test measures." See the following questions for more information on intelligence, and especially Question 8, which discusses Howard Gardner's "Multiple Intelligences."

Question 6: What is the controversy surrounding intelligence?

Dear Dr. Rubin,

One of my friends said there was nothing anyone could do to raise his or her intelligence. In other words, what a person is born with is what he or she has. Many of us disagreed. We got into a very heated discussion concerning intelligence. Finally, I told everyone that I would write to ask you what your thoughts are on this topic.

Sincerely,
Curious Parent

Dear Curious Parent,

The confusion surrounding intelligence may be due to the nature-nurture controversy that has been raging for centuries. Those persons who advocate the nature side of the controversy believe that heredity is the sole determiner of intelligence. They state that the intelligence of a person is set at birth and that no amount of environmental influence can raise it. On the other hand, those persons who believe in the nurture side claim that intelligence is determined by environment, and that it can be raised if the child is exposed to the proper environment and education. However, most professionals today do not take an either/or stance but rather an in-between position; that is, they believe that intelligence is determined by an interaction between heredity and environment. One psychologist aptly stated it this way: "Heredity deals the cards and environment plays them."

The majority position that intelligence is determined by some combination of heredity and environment also has some problems. Psychologists disagree as to which factor is more important—heredity or environment. Conflicting studies present different percentages of importance to each. As of now, the controversy still rages and confusion still exists concerning what intelligence tests measure.

Question 7: What do intelligence tests tell us?

Dear Dr. Rubin,

The whole issue of intelligence testing is very confusing. Our school system has voted to ban group intelligence tests. We'd appreciate hearing your views on this topic.

Sincerely,
Confused Parents

Dear Confused Parents,

Imagine that a child is not well. His parents take him to a doctor for a complete physical. The doctor says to the parents, "I'm sorry, there is one test I would like to use. It would give me needed information, but I can't use it for your child." "Why?" ask the parents. "It's been outlawed in this region," replies the doctor. "That's ridiculous!" cry the parents. And they're correct. This situation, however, does exist in some parts of this country in relation to intelligence testing.

Intelligence testing evokes such emotion that some school systems actually have outlawed the use of group intelligence tests for all their students, and some have even banned individual IQ tests.

Even though there are a variety of tests designed to measure intelligence, no test exists that can actually measure inborn ability. In other words, intelligence tests cannot adequately measure an individual's absolute limits or potential. However, many people, including professionals, behave as if the intelligence test will tell all.

Most intelligence tests are highly verbal and studies have shown that those students who do well on vocabulary tests also seem to do well on intelligence tests. If a child has a language problem—if a child speaks a nonstandard dialect of English or a language other than English is the dominant language at home—the child could have difficulty doing well in school and also on intelligence tests.

Intelligence tests are valid mainly for a middle-class standard English curriculum, and these tests predict the ability of an individual to do well in such school environments. There is a definite relationship between an individual's score on an intelligence test and his or her ability to do work in school. However, it is by no means a perfect relationship. There are other factors besides IQ, which stands for "intelligence quotient" (the score obtained from an intelligence test), that determine an individual's success in school. One very important factor is motivation—the desire, drive, and sustained interest to do the work. Another is home environment.

Intelligence tests do not predict how successful people will be in their careers or in life. Those who finish college often tend to be more successful careerwise than those who do not. However, there are no guarantees. A person with a high IQ will not necessarily make more money than a person with a lower IQ. Factors such as luck, family, and persistence play significant roles. Test constructors caution users that intelligence tests are imperfect tools that should never be used as ends in themselves. And intelligence tests shouldn't be the sole determiner in students' placement.

Teachers should look at the child's performance in class. If children do poorly on an intelligence test but are achieving well in class and on achievement tests, teachers should not conclude that the children are "overachievers." Students cannot achieve more than they are capable of achieving. Perhaps there is something wrong with the test or the children may have been ill when they took the test.

Intelligence tests, properly used, have a place in the schools. They help teachers and parents better understand the abilities of children and are important in identifying those children who may need special help or who are academically gifted. The tests also help teachers recognize that most classes have students with a wide range of ability levels and that teachers must take the individual differences of students into account when planning for instruction.

Intelligence tests should not be outlawed. Nor should they be used as a limiting factor on what any individual can do.

Question 8: What is Howard Gardner's "Multiple Intelligences"?

Dear Dr. Rubin,

I keep hearing people talk about Howard Gardner's "Multiple Intelligences." What are they talking about?

Sincerely,
Curious Parent

Dear Curious Parent,

Howard Gardner's theory in a nutshell is that we are all born with potential to develop various intelligences, which typical intelligence tests do not tap. In other words, intelligence can take on many different forms and functions. Howard Gardner would like schools to reward a broader range of activities that draw on different intelligences. His theory of "Multiple Intelligences" includes different categories such as Logical/Mathematical, Linguistic, Musical, Spatial, Bodily/Kinesthetic, Interpersonal, Intrapersonal, and Naturalist.

It is important to state that others have also come up with different intelligences.

Question 9: How is Howard Gardner's "Multiple Intelligences" being used in some schools?

Dear Dr. Rubin,

Just imagine this: Every day, for 45 minutes, my daughter's teacher has the whole third-grade class gather in a circle to discuss how the students feel about anything that comes to mind. Then the teacher has each child point to another child and praise that child. (The children can also compliment the teacher.) The teacher tells the children that this will make them feel "good." Sara dreads the "I feel good; you feel good; we all feel good" sessions. She can't figure out how you can feel good about doing and achieving nothing. She says that she often just makes up something to say when it's her turn.

Sara's teacher had discussed Gardner's theory of multiple intelligences with her class and had them memorize his different categories. Next, she had the third graders draw an oval, which she told them represents their brain and had them think of how the categories of intelligences would apply to them. Then she had the students divide their oval into the categories according to how they saw themselves, making the one which they felt most applied to them the largest part of their oval.

Sara asked the teacher why they were engaged in this activity. The teacher said that it helped build the students' self-confidence. When I asked the principal the same question my child had asked, the principal said that what they were doing with Howard Gardner's work was at the "cutting edge."

What do you think?

Sincerely,
Frustrated Parent

Dear Frustrated Parent,

Sara's school's use of Howard Gardner's theory is a farce, lacking in any substance. The teacher's practices help "pigeon hole" children and may aid in invoking the self-fulfilling prophecy. If a child isn't good in a certain area, he or she could say, "That's okay, I have ability in another area, so why should I try this one?" Rather than improving students' overall self-concept or developing potential abilities, it's probably hindering their development. It's good that you, as a vigilant parent, aren't allowing school officials to "hoodwink" you.

Teachers should be perceptive to students' needs and sensitive to the varying personalities in their midst; however, teachers aren't psychologists. And it's dangerous for schools to expect them to act as such.

We need schools of education that help prospective teachers understand what their roles as teachers are and that help teachers attain the skills and strategies they must have to become exemplary teachers. We also need administrators who are educational leaders and who recognize inappropriate activities for what they are and eliminate them. And we need lots of vigilant parents such as you.

Question 10: What is the role of the teacher toward academically-gifted children?

Dear Dr. Rubin,

How is it possible for a third grader, who delights in learning and is reading Louisa May Alcott's *Little Women*, to become so frustrated that she rebels at going to school?

My daughter, Rebecca, told me that she wishes she were dumb because then everything would be easier. Rebecca is angry because she claims she already knows everything being done in her class. As a result, her teacher has her tutoring children who need help. Rebecca says she doesn't mind tutoring children who need help, but she minds spending so much time every day doing this. The only new things Rebecca claims she is learning are the spelling words. The students choose the spelling words themselves, so she tries to pick really hard ones to challenge herself.

Rebecca loves science, but there's no organized science program in her class. There isn't even a textbook. At times, her teacher has the children fill out a worksheet on some science-related topics.

Also, when the teacher puts students into cooperative groups, the teacher always chooses Rebecca as discussion leader. (Then she fades into the background.) Each discussion leader has the children read a story aloud, one after the other, and then they give personal responses about the story.

My daughter is very bored. Do you have any suggestions?

Sincerely,
Perplexed Parent

Dear Perplexed Parent,

I am sorry that your daughter is having such frustrating experiences in school. Good teachers provide for the individual differences of all their students. Gifted children, like all children, need guidance and instruction based on their interests, needs, and ability levels. Although gifted children gain abstract concepts quickly and are intellectually capable of working at high levels of abstraction, unless they receive appropriate instruction to gain needed skills, they may not be able to realize their potential. Gifted children should not be subjected to unnecessary drill and repetition. Because they usually enjoy challenge and have long attention spans, teachers need to provide instruction that will challenge and interest them.

Unfortunately, the situation that you relate is possible if the teacher doesn't believe in and doesn't provide any direct instruction and ignores the individual differences of her students. From what you are relating to me, it seems as though your child is an academically highly-able student.

If I were you, I would speak to the teacher and ask her what kinds of enrichment programs she envisions for your daughter that would take into account her precocious learning ability. If you are unhappy with what the teacher says, I would then speak to the principal.

Good Luck!

Question 11: What are the characteristics of academically-gifted students?

ANSWER: Gifted children, on average, are socially, emotionally, physically, and intellectually more advanced than "average" children in the population. These children have, on average, superior general intelligence, a desire to know, originality, common sense, will power and perseverence, a desire to excel, self-confidence and forethought, and a good sense of humor, among other admirable traits. Their language development is usually very advanced. They generally have a large stock of vocabulary and delight in learning new words. Many of these children have learned to read before they come to school; they usually have wide-ranging interests that they pursue in extensive depth, they tend to be voracious readers, and they delight in challenge. However, it is possible that without some guidance, a number of gifted children may not read very challenging books.

Question 12: Why are gifted children sometimes ignored in the classroom?

ANSWER: Gifted children need special attention because of their precocious learning abilities. However, when gifted children are not given special attention, usually they still manage to work on their grade level. As a result, gifted children are often ignored.

Question 13: What helps shape a child's achievement in school?

Dear Dr. Rubin,

We had a discussion last night about the factors that help shape a child's achievement in school. We would appreciate receiving information on this topic.

Sincerely,
Interested Parents

Dear Interested Parents,

The topic you are interested in is one on which volumes of books have been written. I feel that a good way to answer your question is to give you a composite of two children and then ask you to predict, based on the information I present, which child appears to have the best possibilities of achieving in school.

Melissa X	Jim Y
First born	Fifth child of seven children
Two-parent home	One-parent home
Upper-middle class socioeconomic status	Low socioeconomic status—on assistance
College-educated parents	Parent has eighth-grade education
Standard English is dominant language	Nonstandard English is spoken
Parents read to Melissa	Jim is not read to
Child surrounded by books	No books or other print material in sight
Television viewing is supervised	No television supervision
Book and other discussions with parents	No book or other discussions with parent
Parents answer Melissa's questions	Parent gets angry when Jim asks questions
Melissa goes on many trips with parents	Jim stays home
Melissa is supervised	Jim is unsupervised

According to what research suggests, there is no question that Melissa has a good head start and has an excellent chance of succeeding in school.

To help you more, I am sending you some information on concept development and other areas that play a role in children's achievement and success in school.

Question 14: How do children acquire concepts?

ANSWER: The first step in acquiring concepts concerns *vocabulary,* because concepts are based on word meanings: without vocabulary, there would be no concepts because there would be no base for the development of concepts.

The second step in acquiring concepts is *gathering data,* that is, specific information about the concept to be learned. In doing this, children must process information—they must select data that are relevant, ignore irrelevant data, and categorize those items that belong together. Concepts are formed when the data are organized into categories. Let's see how a young child may acquire the concept of the word *pet:*

Andrew is fortunate he lives in a home that is filled with love, kindness, and caring. He also lives in a home that is large enough for pets. Andrew, who is four years old, has a cat, a dog, and fish as pets.

His mother and father use the word *pet* when they refer to the kitty, dog, and fish; they also use the labels *kitty, doggie,* and *fish,* as well as the pets' special names. In Andrew's environment, he has gained a great deal of data concerning pets. He has learned that pets are animals that live in your home; pets, such as dogs and cats, are gentle; and you can play with them. He has also learned that you cannot play with some pets such as fish; these you can only watch. In addition, he has learned that all pets need to be taken care of and that they do not eat the same things.

Andrew, at four, is quite verbal and can tell you a lot about his pets because he has grown up with them. His parents have also talked to him about pets and have read aloud to him many books about animals. Andrew knows that a lion, tiger, elephant, or giraffe would not be pets. He has seen these animals in books and on TV, and he has visited them at the zoo. Andrew has also visited a farm where he has seen such animals as goats, cows, and horses. Andrew knows the difference between tame animals and wild animals. When you talk to him about pets, he can tell you those that would make good pets and those that would not. He laughs when you suggest that he should have an elephant or lion for a pet. He gets hysterical with laughter when you suggest that the cat live in the fishbowl or that the fish should live out of water. He becomes very serious when you recommend that the cat play with the fish. "No, no!" he says, "The cat will eat my fish."

At four, Andrew has gained the concept *pet.* He knows what data to ignore and what data he should include in his concept formation of *pet.* He gained this concept easily because of his background of experiences.

Think for a moment of another four-year-old, however.

Alicia lives in a two-room apartment in the inner city. This four-year-old has five older brothers and sisters. Alicia is the youngest. Her parents both work, and her older sister takes care of her and her brothers and sisters. What kind of information will she gain concerning pets? Where she lives, there are dogs that roam the streets, and you can hear their howls at night. There are also large numbers of cats who must daily forage in the streets for food. When Alicia was two, she was attacked by a dog, and as a result, she is still afraid of any dog. When she sees a rat in the apartment, she runs in fright and tells her sister that she has just seen a "kitty."

Alicia's experiences are certainly different from Andrew's, and this will obviously affect her concept formation of *pet,* a term not even used in her home. The word is not in her listening experience—she doesn't hear that word in use—so Alicia does not have a base or foundation upon which she can adequately build the concept *pet.*

Question 15: Does the home environment play a significant role in how well children do in school?

ANSWER: Children's success in school is usually based on the families into which they are born. Socioeconomic class, parents' education, and the neighborhood in which children live are some of the factors that shape children's home environment. Children who have good, adult language models and who are spoken to and encouraged to speak will have an advantage in the development of language and intelligence. Parents who behave in a warm, democratic manner and provide their children with stimulating, educationally oriented activities, challenge their children to think, encourage independence, and reinforce their children are preparing them very well for school.

Question 16: Does the number of children born into a family, as well as birth order, affect the achievement levels of individuals?

ANSWER: Research is still being done on these factors, but it has been hypothesized that firstborn children usually do better both in school and in life than other children in the family. An only child has been shown to be more articulate for the most part than a child who is the product of a multiple birth, for example, twins or triplets. Also, an only child seems to do better than a child who has other brothers or sisters.

Studies suggest that the only child, who is more often in the company of adults, has more chances of being spoken to by the surrounding grown-ups in the family. Then, too, twins seem to have less need to communicate with others because they have a close relationship.

Children who have other brothers and sisters also have "interpreters" near at hand; that is, older siblings who can often understand a younger child's messages so well that the younger child need not attempt more effective communication.

All of these factors form part of the learning climate in the home and influence the degree and amount of learning in school. The key thing is for parents to recognize the importance of interacting verbally with their children.

Question 17: What is the importance of learning left from right and does a left-handed child have any special problems?

ANSWER: Knowledge of right and left is imperative in order to be able to read and write English effectively. A number of children, especially those who are left-handed, may read the word *saw* for *was* or *was* for *saw* because they are reading from right to left.

To understand better the left-handed child's problem in reading and writing, we must refer to one way in which we all develop. All of us develop from the midpoint of the body to extremities. Because of this, right-handed children move their right hands from left to right naturally. Left-handed children find moving their left hand from left to right against their natural inclination.

Try this simple experiment to illustrate the point: Bring both hands to the center of your body. Now, move both hands out away from your body. The right hand will follow a left-to-right path corresponding to the English pattern of writing; the left hand follows a right-to-left path. If you doubt this, ask any left-hander to write the letter *t*. Observe closely how the left-hander makes the horizontal line for the *t*. Unless the left-hander has been well conditioned, he or she will draw the line from right to left.

It is important to state that just because a child is left-handed does not mean that he or she will necessarily have a reading or handwriting problem. Parents, however, should be aware of the possibility and be on the lookout for reversals in children's reading or writing, that is, the inverting of letters or words. It is normal for many preschoolers to invert letters and words, so parents should not panic if their child does this. However, if a child continues to make reversals when he or she is in the latter part of kindergarten or in first grade, the parent should discuss this with the child's teacher.

Also, it's a good idea for parents to remind the teacher that their child is left-handed so that special attention can be provided, if necessary, as the child is learning to write.

"Simon Says" is a fun game that parents can play with their children to help them distinguish left from right. In this game, parents tell their children to listen carefully because they are going to tell them to do some things, and they must do them exactly the way the parents say. The parents further explain that the children must only follow the directions when they say "Simon Says" before the directions. Then the parents state a number of directions in which their children must discriminate between their left and right hands and feet. After the parents turn, the children make up directions for them.

Here are some sample directions that stress left and right. Of course, the difficulty level will depend on the ages of the children and their attention spans.

1. Simon Says put your right hand on your head and stamp your left foot.
2. Simon Says touch your right leg with your left hand.

Question 18: What is "school phobia"?

ANSWER: This is a confusing concept. However, classic school phobia usually is when a child displaces on the school; that is, the child blames the school for his or her problem, but the problem is actually something that usually stems from the home. A child who has school phobia could say that he or she doesn't want to go to school because of bad things that are happening there, but that is not the "real" reason. Such a child could be unhappy about something at home and, as a result, is fearful about leaving home in the morning. For example, it is could be that there is a new baby in the home, and the child is afraid that the new baby will take his or her place, so the child does not want to go to school.

Question 19: Why do some children get sick every school morning, even though they have no apparent illness?

ANSWER: For a number of parents, school mornings are a nightmare because their children awaken each morning with some kind of ailment. First, it is very important for parents to make sure that their child does not have some serious physical illness. Therefore, it's a good idea to have the child thoroughly checked by a doctor and by specialists, if necessary. If the child continues to get ill on school mornings, it would be wise to check into other possibilities for the child's symptoms.

If the symptoms take place on school mornings only, there may be a relationship between the two. It could be that the child is unhappy about something that is taking place in school, and this is actually making him or her ill. The something could be a multitude of things: the teacher, the child's peers, the classroom situation, and so on. Parents should search for the cause or causes. They should explain the situation to the child's teacher and ask for his or her help. Parents could ask the teacher to observe the child's behavior in school and to note whether their child is under any unusual stress, whether their child is bored or if the work is too difficult. The teacher should also observe whether the child has any friends at school. In addition, parents should talk with their child and try to get the child to pinpoint what the trouble may be. It would be a good idea for parents to try to analyze their behavior toward the child. They must determine if they are making too many demands on their child or if their expectations are too high. In examining their behavior with the child, parents should note whether they are constantly fighting or bickering with one another or with the child. Parents should also analyze the child's relationship with other members of the family.

Another avenue that parents should look into is the school environment and neighborhood in which they live. It could be that the child is being pressured by peers to become involved in situations of which the child disapproves.

Obviously, there are many reasons why a child may get ill in the morning. Parents have a number of channels available to them for help. In addition to speaking to their child's teacher, they should also speak to the school psychologist or to a psychiatrist in private practice.

Parents should persist until the problem is solved. They should not take such pat answers as: "Oh, your child will outgrow it," or "Lots of children go through this phase."

NOTES

100 Q&As *Preschool and Kindergarten*

Question 20: Should parents send their children to preschool?

Dear Dr. Rubin,

My friends and I have a running battle about whether it's better to send children to preschool or keep them home if you are an at-home parent. Please tell us your thoughts on this topic.

> Sincerely,
> At-Home Parent

Dear At-Home Parent,

Your question is asked a lot. As a matter of fact, a parent recently claimed that the parents she knows send their children to preschool, even though many of the mothers are home full time. She said that she felt that if she didn't send her daughter to a preschool, her child would fall behind the other children. She also asked about the kind of preschool I would recommend. She said she was confused because different education experts seem to have opposite views about what is best for young children.

The parent's questions and yours are important ones and highlight the problems that many parents of preschoolers face. The questions about preschools are also coming at a time when reports are continuing to emphasize the importance of the first few years in children's lives. In other words, those children who are exposed at an early age to an intellectually stimulating environment usually do better when they enter school than those who aren't fortunate enough to be in such surroundings. This information isn't news—the first goal of the *Goals 2000: Educate America Act,* which states that children should come to school ready to learn, is based on research that shows the positive effects of preschoolers being exposed to a print-rich environment.

There is, however, no hard and fast rule that says all children must attend preschool. Years ago, most preschoolers stayed home until it was time to go to kindergarten. Some parents may have sent their preschoolers to a nursery school because they felt it would be a good experience for their children, especially if their children didn't have any playmates close by. Most nursery schools they went to were places where children played a lot and had "fun."

If a parent is home and exposes the preschooler to various kinds of stimulating intellectually-oriented activities, the child obviously doesn't have to attend preschool. If parents feel, however, that their children will lose out if they aren't in preschool and if the parents can afford the cost, they often enroll their children.

Once parents have decided to send their children to preschool, they have to decide on the kind of program they want them to have. This isn't easy because many educators don't agree on the kinds of programs young children should receive. Here's where parental input is imperative because parents know their children best.

Most individuals interpret an intellectually stimulating environment for young children to be one in which they are exposed to a great amount of print material and are read to. However, today, educators such as E.D. Hirsch, Jr., are saying that since research suggests that young children's brains are the most ripe for learning, more should be done to stimulate them academically at that time. Some other educators agree and also blast the kinds of nonacademic programs that a number of preschools presently have.

Many preschool programs are permissive ones that believe it's best to allow children to "develop naturally" without external interference. In other words, even though children would be immersed in lots of print, nothing much, for example, may be done to directly help children learn the relationship between the spoken word and the printed one or to help children gain comprehension skills. Many educators still feel preschool should primarily be a permissive, fun-filled environment where teachers read aloud to children, and where there's lots of playtime, art projects, sharing time, and other similar kinds of activities.

The good news is that different kinds of preschools are available from which parents can choose. Interestingly, many parents seem to be choosing those preschools that are more academically-oriented.

Parents must be careful, however, that they don't turn off preschoolers from school before they start. It's one thing to provide them with a stimulating intellectual environment; it's quite another to put young preschoolers into a highly structured pressure-cooker environment that could rob them of the joys of childhood. Preschools shouldn't be mini-first grades, and, very importantly, neither should first grades be mini-preschools. The key is to get young children hooked on wanting to learn. However, balance must prevail.

The bottom line is that each parent will have to decide what is best for his or her child. There is no one best answer for all.

Question 21: What is the "Parent Checklist for Preschoolers"?

This is a diagnostic tool that lists some of the things that parents should be doing with their preschoolers. It's a good idea to periodically check the list to see how well you are faring.

Child's Name _____ Date _____

Parent Checklist for Preschoolers

- ☐ I listen to my child.

- ☐ I read aloud to my child.

- ☐ I have my child make predictions about the story.

- ☐ I ask my child lots of "why" questions related to the story.

- ☐ I have my child recall the story.

- ☐ I have my child read picture books to me.

- ☐ I watch TV shows with my child.

- ☐ I talk about the TV shows with my child.

- ☐ I discuss things with my child.

- ☐ I spend time with my child.

- ☐ I ask my child good questions.

- ☐ I am patient with my child.

- ☐ I take my child to interesting places.

- ☐ I do not over-structure my child's life.

- ☐ I do not pressure my child.

- ☐ I read and write in the presence of my child.

- ☐ I am a good role model for my child.

Question 22: What are some suggestions for reading stories aloud to young children?

Dear Dr. Rubin,

I would be very grateful if you would please send me some suggestions for reading stories aloud to my children. I want to give my preschoolers every advantage I can.

Sincerely,
Grateful Parent

Dear Grateful Parent,

Reading stories aloud to young children is an essential activity for building the knowledge and skills eventually required for reading. It can be a wonderful, interactive learning experience if it is done properly. Here are a few steps that will ensure success.

First, choose a storybook that is at the attention, interest, and concept-development level of your child. Make sure that the story has pictures related to the story. Before you begin reading the story aloud, have your child make predictions about the story. As you are reading the story aloud, stop at key points and have your child predict what he or she thinks will happen next. Your child also could state the refrain if the story contains one. In addition, you could state some questions for your child to think about while you are reading aloud. If your child interjects comments during the story, acknowledge these by saying "good thinking" if it shows that he or she is thinking, and then continue reading.

After you have finished reading the story and discussed whether your child's predictions were correct, have your child answer the unanswered questions and do some of the following activities based on his or her attention and interest levels:

	Tell what the story is about
	Retell the story in sequence
	Discuss whether the story is "make-believe" or not
	Act out the story
	Make up another ending for the story

Question 23: Should a child interrupt when a parent reads aloud to him or her?

Dear Dr. Rubin,

Should a child interrupt when a parent reads aloud to him or her? This question has always bothered me. My friends say they don't allow their children to interrupt when they read aloud to their children. I, however, do. Am I wrong?

Sincerely,
Confused Parent

Dear Confused Parent,

You are not alone in your confusion on this issue. Interestingly enough, studies suggest that allowing children to interact with the reader and story will help them to be more actively involved and become better thinkers and readers. This practice is superior to their merely sitting still and listening. After all, how do you know that children are listening well unless you get feedback from them?

Question 24: What kinds of books should I read aloud to my preschooler?

Dear Dr. Rubin,

Could you suggest some kinds of books I should read to my preschooler?

Sincerely,
Curious Parent

Dear Curious Parent,

It's a good idea to choose books to read aloud to preschoolers, such as *The Little Red Hen,* that have continuous refrains; that is, the story keeps repeating similar passages. Children love these type of books; they enjoy saying the refrain. When reading the book aloud, it's a good idea for parents to stop before the refrain and let the child say it. It's also a good idea for parents to reinforce a child's response with encouraging words after the child states the refrain, even if what the child says isn't exactly word for word.

Chicka Chicka Boom Boom by Bill Martin, Jr. and John Archambault (Simon & Schuster) is a delightful alphabet rhyme book that children usually love. *Goodnight Moon* by Margaret Wise Brown (HarperCollins) is also a beloved book of most children. Children also especially like books such as Margaret Wise Brown's *Noisy* books (HarperCollins). Even though Brown's books were written years ago, almost every library includes her gems in their collection.

Brown's *The Noisy Book* is about a little dog named Muffin, who hears all kinds of noises. Her *Country Noisy Book* is also about the little dog, who goes to the country for the first time and hears all kinds of country sounds. In *The Indoor Noisy Book,* Muffin has a cold and spends the whole day inside.

All of the Margaret Wise Brown books lend themselves to interaction by the children. Parents can encourage their children to supply the appropriate sound while looking at the pictures.

Because young children especially love sound books, here are a few that your children will probably enjoy:

Crash! Bang! Boom! and *Gobble, Growl, Grunt,* both by Peter Spier (Doubleday); *The Listening Walk* by Paul Showers (HarperCollins); *Good-Night Owl!* by Pat Hutchins (Macmillan); *Hoot Howl Hiss* by Michelle Koch (Greenwillow Books); *Country Crossing* by Jim Aylesworth (Atheneum); *Polar Bear, Polar Bear, What Do You Hear?* by Bill Martin, Jr. and Eric Carle (Henry Holt); *Barnyard Banter* by Denise Fleming (Henry Holt); *Wheel Away!* by Dayle Ann Dodds (Harper & Row).

Question 25: Is it normal for a child to want the same book read over and over again?

Dear Dr. Rubin,

My child likes me to read a story over and over again. Is this normal?

Sincerely,
Concerned Parent

Dear Concerned Parent,

Yes, yes, yes it's normal. Children love to hear their favorite stories reread a number of times. It makes them feel secure and safe when they revisit a book they enjoy. Parents may get tired of reading the same book innumerable times, but not children.

Question 26: What kinds of questions should I ask my child about the story that I am reading aloud?

Dear Dr. Rubin,

What kinds of questions should I ask my child about the story I am reading aloud to her?

Sincerely,
Curious Parent

Dear Curious Parent,

Your question is a very important one. Research suggests that parents who ask many questions that begin with "why" are helping their children more than those who ask most of their questions beginning with "what." The "why" questions encourage children to think beyond the literal level where answers are directly stated. It requires children to do more higher-level thinking. Good question-askers should use a combination of both "what" and "why" questions.

Question 27: When is a child ready for kindergarten?

Dear Dr. Rubin,

When is a child ready for kindergarten? My husband and I are confused about what to do concerning our son whose birthday is in August. The cutoff day for kindergarten is September 1, which means he would be one of the youngest in the class.

Sincerely,
Confused Parents

Dear Confused Parents,

This is a difficult question to answer. Many parents are upset because they live in school districts where the cutoff date for entry into kindergarten is one day away from their child's birthday. For example, read the following:

Leslie and Anna have been friends since they were babies. The two little girls have done almost everything together and even gone to the same preschool. For the first time, however, all this will change because Anna will start kindergarten in the fall, but Leslie will not. Even though Anna and Leslie are only one day apart in chronological age, Anna is considered ready for school, whereas Leslie isn't. The reason is simple. Anna was born on September 30, whereas Leslie was born on October 1. The cutoff date for school entry in the girls' school district is September 30.

Readiness in Anna and Leslie's school district is determined by a cutoff date. And this practice isn't unique to this school district.

The controversy concerning cutoff dates for starting kindergarten isn't new, and many early childhood educators claim they are tired of debating the same old question about kindergarten cutoff dates.

Leslie's parents have decided to send their child to a private pre-kindergarten pre-school, which presents a program similar to the kindergarten program Anna will be receiving in her public school kindergarten class. Leslie's parents feel that their daughter, who has had many experiences with print material and can already read many words and loves books, would be bored if she were placed in a kindergarten next year rather than first grade. And since Leslie missed the cutoff date by just one day, they feel their decision is justified.

However, what is "right" for Leslie is not necessarily "right" for your son. When a child is ready for school depends on a number of factors. You can use the School Entry Questionnaire (see Question 28) to help you decide if your child is ready for school.

Good Luck.

Question 28: What is the "School Entry Questionnaire"?

ANSWER: The School Entry Questionnaire may help you decide whether your child is ready for school. If you answer "yes" to all or most of the questions (see next page for the School Entry Questionnaire), I suggest that you discuss your child's situation with the school personnel in your school district.

It is especially important to meet with the school personnel in your district if your child has missed the school entry cutoff date, but he or she is already reading and you have answered "yes" to most of the questions on the School Entry Questionnaire.

Child's Name _____ Date _____

School Entry Questionnaire

	Yes	No
1. Does your child have a good attention span; that is, can he or she listen for an extended period of time?		
2. Does your child enjoy looking at picture books?		
3. Can your child make inferences about the pictures; that is, if the children are wearing jackets, hats, gloves, and pants, can he or she answer a question such as: What kind of a day is it?		
4. Can your child recognize letters?		
5. Does your child want to learn to read?		
6. Does your child read road signs and words on cereal boxes?		
7. Does your child ask you to tell him or her a word on a page?		
8. Does your child remember the word you told him or her and point it out to you?		
9. Can your child listen to a story and answer some questions about it?		
10. Can your child listen to a story and retell it in sequence?		
11. Does your child know how to count?		
12. Does your child realize that the number *one* stands for *one* thing, the number *two* stands for *two* things, and so on?		
13. Does your child want to learn to write?		
14. Does your child like to write; that is, does he or she ask you for paper and pencils or crayons, and does your child attempt to write his or her name?		
15. Can your child draw a square?		
16. Can your child draw a person, and does she or he include details in the drawing?		
17. Can your child use scissors well?		
18. Can your child follow directions?		

© FEARON TEACHER AIDS FE21100

	Yes	No
19. Does your child have a good speaking vocabulary?		
20. Does your child have many words in his or her listening experience; that is, does he or she know the meaning of words when they are said aloud?		
21. Does your child express himself or herself well?		
22. Is your child logical in discussions with you or friends?		
23. Can your child hold his or her own with friends who are entering school?		
24. Does your child say to you that he or she wants to go to school?		

NOTES

Question 29: Why do some parents choose to keep children out of kindergarten an extra year?

Dear Dr. Rubin,

My husband and I are debating whether to keep our son out of kindergarten for an extra year. How do you feel about this?

Sincerely,
Totally Confused Parents

Dear Totally Confused Parents,

A number of parents just like you have struggled with the same issue. In other words, some parents, even if their children are within the kindergarten school entry range date, keep their children out of school an extra year to supposedly give them an advantage. The reasoning is that older children will do better because they are developmentally more advanced than younger children. The studies in this area aren't too helpful because they tend to contradict one another. Some researchers claim that younger children in the class usually score lower on achievement tests than older ones and that these children are more prone to need special education services, become discipline problems, and repeat a grade. Other researchers agree that some younger children may score lower than their older peers; however, the achievement disparity is rather small and they claim that by third grade the differences disappear. Still others disagree with the latter findings and claim that children who, in first grade, don't become six until January 1st have problems until sixth grade. Investigators also suggest strongly that younger boys more so than girls appear to have long-term problems in school.

Parents know their children best. If you have a son who is immature for his age and who would be one of the youngest in his kindergarten class, you may opt to keep him out for another year while, at the same time, filling his year with rich literacy experiences. If, however, you have a child who would be one of the youngest in the class but who is advanced for his or her age and has been exposed to lots of print, you probably should consider enrolling this child in kindergarten. It all boils down to what is best for the individual child.

On page 32 is the School Entry Questionnaire that you can use to help you decide whether your child is ready for school. If you answer "yes" to all the questions, I suggest that you discuss your child's situation with the school personnel in your school district. Remember, too, that you as the parents know your child best.

I hope this helps you.

Question 30: What are the states' entry dates for kindergarten?

Dear Dr. Rubin,

Do all the states have the same kindergarten entry dates? We're confused about this.

Sincerely,
Confused Parents

Dear Confused Parents,

Join the club—there are a lot of other parents just as confused. States differ as to their cutoff dates for entry to kindergarten, so I cannot give you any specific dates. It might interest you to know, however, that in 1997, school attendance for five-year-olds was only mandatory in seven states and the District of Columbia, and twelve states, including the District of Columbia, mandated full-day kindergarten for their children. The other states required half-day kindergarten, unless stipulated differently by individual school boards. In those states where school boards can determine what kind of program to provide for students based on available monies, parents either pay for private kindergartens or wait until first grade to enroll their children in public school.

A number of school districts have recently incorporated full-day kindergartens for the children in their school districts. As of the writing of this book, this is still more the exception than the norm.

Those states that are considering moving their kindergarten school entry date from September 1st to June 1st, so that children entering kindergarten will supposedly be older, are meeting with resistance. The fly in the ointment is that whatever the cutoff date is, there will always be children who are older and those who are younger. A child born on June 2nd who isn't allowed entry to kindergarten because of the cutoff date would be a year older than the June 1st child. Also, even if children were the exact same chronological age, there would still be developmental differences among the children because of various individual differences. In other words, two children of similar chronological age may be months and even years apart mentally, socially, and emotionally.

Check with your school district for kindergarten entry dates in your area.

Question 31: What is the difference between "reading readiness" and "emergent literacy"?

Dear Dr. Rubin,

When I went to school, teachers talked about reading readiness. Today, I keep hearing the term *emergent literacy*. Please explain the differences, if there are any. Also, what are reading readiness tests and what are they supposed to measure?

Thank you.

Sincerely,
Perplexed Parent

Dear Perplexed Parent,

The term *reading readiness* has been replaced by that of *emergent literacy*. *Emergent literacy* is, however, a much broader concept than *reading readiness*. The term *emergent literacy* connotes an ongoing process, whereas the term *reading readiness,* which was prevalent for a long time in the field of reading, seems to connote a *waiting period.* The idea of a *waiting period* in literacy development violates the spirit or essence of literacy as a developmental process; therefore it is not surprising that there has been a shift away from the concept of reading readiness to emergent literacy.

Reading readiness usually has been referred to as the experiences that children received in kindergarten or the beginning of first grade before formal reading began. The term has had negative connotations attached to it because if a child did poorly on a reading readiness test, the children were usually delayed from entering a formal reading program.

Deleting or changing terms, however, will not change practices.

Today we talk about levels of literacy and recognize that an individual's literacy is something that continues all through life. Emergent literacy is that stage in the literacy continuum that deals with the child's developing literacy. Even though agreement doesn't exist on a definition of *emergent literacy*, many educators define it as that stage in the literacy continuum before conventional reading and writing begin. It refers to the "reading" and "writing" experiences that children have before they enter school or before formal or conventional reading and writing take place.

Today, we usually use the term *pre-reading tests* rather than *reading readiness tests*. These pre-reading tests are supposed to predict when children are "ready" to begin a formal reading program. Regardless of which term is used, the concept of delaying reading instruction until a child is ready has always been and still is for most educators an insupportable position because readiness is ongoing.

Question 32: What has led the television industry to provide ratings for their shows?

Dear Dr. Rubin,

My husband and I know that protecting our nation's children from violence has led to ratings for television shows. Who, however, has been responsible for the ratings? And are we the only ones who are unhappy with them?

Sincerely yours,
Inquisitive Parents

Dear Inquisitive Parents,

As you know, parents are concerned about the kinds of material their children, and especially their young impressionable children, are exposed to. Parents' concern about the violence, sexual content, and language of films led the movie industry in 1968 to appoint a committee headed by Jack Valenti to rate movies. The movie ratings were met with mixed reviews but were primarily accepted by most parents. Valenti's recent television ratings haven't fared as well. Parents, to their credit, want more substantive information about the shows' content rather than some age-appropriate rating designated by Valenti and his committee. The television rating battle is still raging. I guess you are not alone in your unhappiness with the ratings.

Question 33: What effect, if any, does violence in fairy tales have on young children?

Dear Dr. Rubin,

I've been wondering about the violence prevalent in many well-known fairy tales. Could you please tell me your thoughts on this in relation to young children?

Sincerely,
Wondering Parent

Dear Wondering Parent,

Parents may not realize that they may be promoting fear and confusion in their preschoolers' minds when they read aloud familiar fairy tales, such as "Little Red Riding Hood," to their young children.

In the Brothers Grimm version, a little girl dressed in a red coat and hood is sent by her mother to bring some food to her ill grandmother who lives deep in the forest. As the child, Little Red Riding Hood, walks along the path to her grandmother's house, she meets a wolf.

Little Red Riding Hood doesn't know that the friendly sounding wolf is actually very wicked. The cunning wolf discovers where the little girl is going, gets there before her, devours the grandmother, tricks Little Red Riding Hood into thinking he is the grandmother, and then gobbles her up, too. The wolf, feeling very full, falls asleep. A hunter, passing by, hears the wolf's loud snoring. He goes inside the house, sees the wolf, and rather than shoot him, cuts open the wolf's stomach. Then out leaps Little Red Riding Hood followed by her grandmother.

The hunter and Little Red Riding Hood fill the wolf's stomach with stones, and the grandmother sews up the opening. The wolf, awakens, drags himself home feeling heavy and uncomfortable. At home, he falls down and never gets up again. And that's the end of the wicked wolf.

In this classic tale of warning, it isn't hard to figure out that the big bad wolf personifies the big bad stranger. The child is being warned about being too trusting of strangers and of speaking to them. The problem is that most preschoolers are at a literal level cognitively, so the "moral" of the tale may be completely lost on many of them. Consequently, the "warning tale" may become merely a "frightening tale" so that young children might look upon all new people and situations as dangerous or scary.

Even though parents tell their children that the story Little Red Riding Hood is just a make-believe story, there's lots of gore and violence in this tale. Also, based on the content of the story, think of how confusing it could be to young children.

Parents should recognize that different versions of the same story exist and determine the kind of message they want to convey to their children. Fairy tales can be read for a moral message, as a tale of warning, or, based on the fairy tale, for the sheer joy of the story.

Parents know their young children. For some children, the big bad wolf or wicked witch will produce nightmares; for others they may not. It makes sense that parents should be especially careful about reading aloud any story at bedtime that is too stimulating for their children. Parents should also freely change or delete any words, sentences, or even endings that might frighten their children.

Whatever story parents read aloud, they must be careful that they aren't planting monsters in their children's minds that will be difficult to erase in future years.

P.S. It might interest you to know that the Japanese take a different stance toward fairy tales such as "Little Red Riding Hood." In one Japanese version, while the wolf is napping, a hunter also happens by, cuts open the wolf's stomach, and frees both Little Red Riding Hood and her grandmother. They also fill the wolf's stomach with stones. The similarity, however, ends here. In the Japanese version, the wolf, rather than dying, feels ill and is filled with remorse for what he has done. He apologizes for his wicked deeds to Little Red Riding Hood and her grandmother and promises to mend his ways.

The Japanese use adapted versions of tales, such as Little Red Riding Hood, to achieve their goal of socialization, preparing an individual to live in society. The Japanese want to drive home moral messages that concentrate on helping young people live virtuous and harmonious lives. Apologizing for wrongful acts and making up with those who have been hurt are key lessons the Japanese would like their tales to teach.

NOTES

 Reading

Question 34: When should children learn to read?

Dear Dr. Rubin,
My friends and I are confused because we learned to read in first grade, but the teachers in our school district keep saying that children will learn to read if they are immersed in enough print. They also claim that their role is to "step back" and let the children learn "naturally." What are they talking about?
   Sincerely,
   Totally Confused Parents

Dear Totally Confused Parents,
I agree that there has been and still is a lot of confusion in the field of reading. However, on average, children can and should learn to read in first grade. Some politicians, rather than stressing that children should learn to read in first grade, are stating as their goal that children should learn to read by the time they finish third grade. And some literacy standards are even stating that children should learn to read by the end of fourth grade.

Parents, however, are correct in wanting their children to learn to read in first grade. Learning to read in first grade is essential because studies suggest strongly that, on average, the longer children remain nonreaders, the more difficult it is for them to reach their grade levels, let alone their ability levels.

Your child appears to be in a whole language classroom. This is interesting because we are supposedly emerging from the era of whole language. Today the emphasis is on a balanced reading program. However, if teachers haven't gained the skills to present a balanced reading program, they will obviously not be able to do so. Such teachers will continue doing what they were doing before. And it appears that this is what is happening in your child's class.

Whole language is a philosophy. It is a set of beliefs about how reading should be taught. This philosophy is based on the assumption that if children are immersed in "good" literature, they will gain all the skills they need to learn how to read. Whole language teachers believe that by reading aloud to children and having a whole class read aloud together, children will gain needed reading skills.

Many whole language teachers don't believe in direct instruction. They see their role as facilitators—as individuals who "get out of the children's way."

For years, studies have reported how important it is for children to learn to read in first grade. The point is that no matter how many stories people read aloud to children, most usually will not learn to read unless they receive direct, systematic instruction in learning to read.

What's disconcerting is that many teachers have graduated from schools of education that haven't presented them with a balanced approach to the teaching of reading. Consequently, numerous primary-grade teachers presently lack the skills and strategies they need to help their students learn to read. And suspect practices, such as the teaching of reading to a whole class are still occurring.

To have most first-graders reading in first grade, all first-grade teachers must be well versed in teaching reading and in how to incorporate a diagnostic-reading and correction program in their classrooms.

There are a number of things that you as parents can do. First, you must make sure that you are providing your children with a home environment where your children are surrounded by print. Studies suggest strongly that preschool children who come from homes where they are read to and are developing many language skills usually do better in school than those who don't have these experiences.

What you as parents also can do is to voice your opinions at Parent Teacher Association (PTA) meetings, to teachers, principals, the superintendent, and especially to school board members. Remember, there is power in collective voices.

P.S. I am including for your information a question and answer guide on reading (beginning on page 41) that you might find interesting.

Question and Answer Guide on Reading

Question 35: What is the definition of reading?

ANSWER: Alonzo is able to read aloud all the words in a passage; however, he cannot answer any questions about the passage. Is he reading? Shurae makes a few errors when she reads aloud; however, the errors she makes do not seem to prevent her from answering any of the questions about the passage. Is she reading? Sarah reads a passage on something about which she has very strong feelings; she has difficulty answering the questions based on the passage because of her attitude. Is Sarah reading? Keenan can figure out all the words in the passage and he thinks he knows their meanings; however, he cannot answer the questions about the passage. Is Keenan reading?

The answers to the questions just posed are based on our definition of reading. There is no single, set definition of reading. As a result, it is difficult to define it simply. A broad definition that has been greatly used is that *reading is a complex process that involves the bringing of meaning to and the taking of meaning from the printed page.* This definition implies that readers bring their backgrounds, their experiences, as well as their emotions, into play when they are reading.

A reader who is upset or physically ill will bring these feelings into the act of reading and this could interfere with the interpretive process. A person well versed in what he or she is reading about will gain more from the reading material than one less knowledgeable. A person who is a good critical reader will gain more when reading a passage dealing with critical thinking than one who is not. A reader who has strong dislikes will come away with different feelings and understandings than a student with strong likes.

If reading is defined as a *complex process that involves the bringing of meaning to and the taking of meaning from the printed page;* then Shurae is actually the only one who is reading because she is the only one who understands what she is reading.

Reading is a thinking act; without thinking, there is no understanding, and without understanding, there is no reading. With this in mind, let's look at the other children we met earlier. Although Alonzo can verbalize all the words in the passage, he has no comprehension of what he is reading; therefore he is not reading. Sarah also can verbalize the words, but her strong feelings about the topic in the selection has prevented her from getting the message the writer is conveying. She is not reading. Keenan can figure out all the words and knows the meanings of the individual words, but either he is not able to get the sense of the passage or he does not know the meanings of the words in another context. He is not reading.

It is important to state that *word recognition* is the foundation of reading and necessary for comprehension, but having word recognition does not guarantee that reading comprehension will take place. Again, without understanding, there is no reading.

Question 36: What is a balanced reading program?

ANSWER: A *balanced reading program* is one that incorporates the best of whole language with a sequential development of word recognition skills. It also focuses on fostering a love of reading in children so that they become life-long readers.

In a balanced reading program, teachers use a mix of materials and methods to help their students learn to read. They also incorporate flexible grouping. In other words, students can move freely from one group to another based on their needs. Teachers in such programs work with the whole class, with small groups, with large groups, and with individual students based on what is appropriate for the lesson being presented.

Question 37: Is it possible for children to understand something when it is read aloud but not when they are reading it themselves?

ANSWER: Yes. Reading diagnosticians recognize that there are children who have excellent comprehension ability but they cannot decode the words on the printed page. A good way to determine whether children have good comprehension is to read a passage aloud to them and then ask them questions about the passage.

Question 38: What is word recognition?

ANSWER: *Word recognition* is a twofold process, which deals with the identification of a word in some way so that individuals can pronounce it, and the association of meaning to the word.

Question 39: What are some word recognition strategies?

ANSWER: Word recognition is composed of various pronunciation and word meaning strategies. The pronunciation strategy that helps children become self-reliant readers is phonics—learning the relationship between letters and the sounds they represent. Other pronunciation strategies are: learning whole word pronunciation, asking someone how words are pronounced, structural analysis and synthesis of words (breaking down and building up of word parts), and using a dictionary to determine pronunciation. The meaning strategies are: using context clues to discern word meaning, asking someone else the meaning of a word, using a dictionary to discern meaning, and structural analysis and synthesis.

Question 40: Why do some children lack word recognition skills?

ANSWER: It could be due to educative or noneducative factors. It could be that the child has never been helped to gain a sequential development of word recognition skills. It could also be noneducative factors that are preventing the child from decoding words on the printed page. For example, it could be that the child has a visual or auditory problem about which the parents are unaware.

Question 41: How can parents determine if their children are "really" reading?

ANSWER: In some classrooms today, children act as though they are reading when, in essence, they are only mimicking what they have heard. Such classes have choral reading rather than reading lessons. When children have heard a story a number of times, they often memorize it. Memorizing a story is not reading it. Parents can take words out of the context of the story and see if the children can state what they are.

Question 42: What are some educational reasons for children *not* learning to read in first grade?

ANSWER: Even though the teaching emphasis presently is on a balanced reading approach, extreme whole language advocates are prevalent in schools because it's often hard for people to change when they have invested so much time and effort in their cause to the exclusion of other philosophies. In these extreme whole language classrooms, teachers believe that their role is to "step back" and get out of the children's way. They believe that if children are immersed in enough reading and writing, they will eventually learn to read. Unfortunately, "eventually" comes too late for many children and is often much too little for others. In many classrooms even today, numerous teachers teach reading to their whole class. And the reading lesson, which is really more of a choral speaking activity, often consists of the teacher and all the children reading aloud together or the children reading aloud along with a tape of the book.

Question 43: What is the role of children reading aloud?

ANSWER: Much can be learned about a child's reading abilities by listening to him or her read aloud. And when children are learning to read, they read aloud a lot. But how can teachers tell whether a child knows how to pronounce words on the printed page if everyone is reading aloud together? Obviously, they can't. There is definitely a role for children reading aloud in a reading lesson. In a directed reading lesson, teachers should have children read aloud for a purpose. In other words, after the children have answered questions about what they have read, the teacher or parent should have the children act as detectives and find clues in their reading that support their answers. Now, children have a purpose for reading aloud. And while the child reads aloud, good teachers listen carefully to note any word recognition problems the child may have.

Question 44: Is oral reading more important than silent reading?

ANSWER: Both oral and silent reading are important. After first graders have learned to decode some printed words, they should begin to read silently for a purpose. And if children have difficulty answering questions after reading silently, teachers need to determine if their students have a word recognition or comprehension problem. However, in some classrooms, in the early grades, it's often difficult to find any directed silent reading activities.

Question 45: What can be done to help children in the early grades gain the skills they need to become effective readers?

ANSWER: Presently many school districts spend lots of money on training some teachers to work in a one-on-one, skill-based reading program with a few first graders who are experiencing extreme difficulty in learning to read. Early intervention, however, is imperative for all children, and all first graders need to gain the skills necessary to make them self-reliant readers. Therefore, all elementary teachers, and especially first-grade teachers, must be knowledgeable of the techniques to teach reading to all their students.

Question 46: What can parents do to have input in the school's reading program?

ANSWER: If enough parents voice their dissatisfaction with extremes that still exist in some schools in the teaching of beginning reading, and if enough phone to request teachers who believe in helping children gain a sequential development of skills, wise administrators will pay attention, especially with vouchers nipping at public schools' heels.

Question 47: What is the place of phonics in a school's reading program?

ANSWER: *Phonics* is a decoding technique. It is a method to teach the relationship between letters and the sounds they represent. Phonics, which deals purely with the pronunciation of words, is important because in learning to read it helps students become more independent readers.

Please note, however that phonics is one part of word recognition, which itself is one part of the reading process. This is being stressed so that you recognize that balance is the key and that extremes usually don't work. Word recognition is the foundation of reading, but without comprehension, there is no reading. Obviously, for reading to take place, there must be both word recognition (see Questions 38 and 39) and comprehension.

Question 48: What kinds of phonics skills should children be learning in school?

Dear Dr. Rubin,

I would appreciate it very much if you would send me the kinds of phonics skills my children should be learning in school.

Sincerely yours,
Appreciative Parent

Dear Appreciative Parent,

I am sending you a sequential development of phonics skills according to levels, that children in kindergarten through grade three should be gaining in school. I am presenting these in levels, but the amount of information children should receive is based on their individual differences. If possible, sit down with your child's teacher and go over this list of skills to ensure that your child is gaining these phonics skills.

Phonics: Skills for Grades K–3

Level One

Auditory discrimination
Visual discrimination
Alphabet recognition

Level Two

Review of auditory and visual discrimination
Consonants
Initial consonants
Final consonants
Vowels
Recognition of long vowel sounds
Recognition of short vowel sounds
Vowel generalizations
Long vowel generalizations
Short vowel generalizations
The final silent "e"
Word families (phonograms)—*an, at, et, un, all,* and *ake*

Level Three

Consonants

    Review of initial and final single consonants

    Consonant blends

        Initial consonant blends

        Final consonant blends

    Consonant digraphs

        Initial consonant digraphs

        Final consonant digraphs

    Silent consonants

Vowels

    Review of long vowel sounds, short vowel sounds, and
        some vowel generalizations

    Vowel digraphs

    Diphthongs

Word families (phonograms)—*ag, ain, am, ame, ay, en,* and *ick*

Level Four

Special letters and sounds

    "Y"

    "C" and "G"

    "Q"

    "R"

    The schwa (ə)

Syllabication

    Phonics applied to syllabicating words

    Introducing accenting

Word families (phonograms)–*ap, ate, ing, ill, ent, est, in,* and *y* (long *i* family)

Question 49: What kinds of comprehension skills should children be learning in school?

Dear Dr. Rubin,

Please send me a list of the kinds of comprehension skills my child should be receiving in school.

    Sincerely,
    Appreciative Parent

Dear Appreciative Parent,
I am attaching a list of some of the kinds of comprehension skills your child should get in school. I hope this helps.

Comprehension Skills for Grades K–3:

Finding information directly stated in text

Drawing inferences—"Reading between the lines"

Cause and effect

Finding the main idea of a paragraph

Finding the central idea of a story

Following directions

Categorizing

Completing word relationships

Finding inconsistencies

Distinguishing between fantasy and reality

Distinguishing between fact and opinion

Recognizing some propaganda techniques

Using divergent thinking

Question 50: What is the relationship of vocabulary to reading?

Dear Dr. Rubin,

What is the relationship between vocabulary and reading?

Sincerely,
Curious Parent

Dear Curious Parent,

A good vocabulary and good reading go hand-in-hand. Unless students know the meaning of words they will have difficulty in understanding what they are reading. Acquiring word meaning is an important skill that should continue not only through school but all through life. Studies strongly suggest that vocabulary is an important factor in reading comprehension and also on tests of academic aptitude. In addition, it is has been found that poor readers generally have smaller vocabularies than good readers.

I am attaching a list of some vocabulary skills that children should be receiving in school. Please note that children usually enjoy working with word riddles and word puzzles, which also help children increase their vocabulary. I hope this information helps.

Vocabulary Skills for Grades K–3:

Using context clues to determine word meanings

Expanding vocabulary with words that have the same or nearly the same meaning (synonyms) and words opposite in meaning (antonyms)

Expanding vocabulary using words with multiple meanings (homographs)

Question 51: **What should be done for a child who learned to read before kindergarten?**

Dear Dr. Rubin,

We are at our wit's end. We have a very bright, articulate child who learned to read before he went to kindergarten. We were told by neighbors that the school he is enrolled in is supposed to be excellent. We decided to send Seth to kindergarten with his age peers because we thought it was important for him to advance socially and emotionally, as well as intellectually. We now fear that we were wrong. Seth is bored. He is already reading, but the teacher is first working with the letters of the alphabet and numbers. Seth reads with understanding. He loves science and enjoys working with numbers. He needs a stimulating, enriched environment.

We've spoken to the teacher and the principal. They keep telling my husband and myself how important it is for Seth to learn to get along with others. We agree. But we also feel that they should take his individual differences into account. He seems to be marking time in school. We would appreciate hearing your thoughts on this topic.

Sincerely,
Disenchanted Parents

Dear Disenchanted Parents,

Your son sounds as though he is academically gifted.

Academically gifted children score significantly above the "average" and need special attention because of their precocious learning abilities. Unfortunately, gifted students are often ignored. Consequently, gifted children generally have to fend for themselves, aren't adequately challenged, and, in many classrooms, become "put-upon" students, that is, they spend most of the day tutoring other children.

Parents of academically gifted children should be ever vigilant that the traditional public schools are providing gifted students with the guidance and instruction they need based on their interests, needs, and ability levels.

I salute you for being vigilant, caring parents. I suggest you talk again about your concerns with the teacher, especially about a special enrichment program for your son. If you are still dissatisfied, it would be a good idea to talk again to the principal of your school. In addition, I would find out what special provisions are provided for academically gifted children in your school system. It may be that you will have to change your child's class and move him to one where the teacher is more capable of dealing with academically-able children.

Question 52: Why do some children from good home backgrounds *not* learn how to read?

Dear Dr. Rubin,

Do you know of any cases where a child seems to "have it all," yet he is not learning to read? We are confused about what is happening to our child. He's having a terrible time in first grade learning to read and we notice that he's changing from a happy young person to a brooding, sad one. Please write to us about any experiences you have had that might relate to our son.

Sincerely yours,
Parents at the End of their Rope

Dear Parents,
The following case study is one that may have some relevance to your child. Remember, however, that each child is unique and that I cannot diagnose any child's difficulties unless I have observed and assessed the child.

Jonathan (a pseudonym) is a blonde, blue-eyed child who comes from an upper-middle class home and has highly educated, caring parents. Jonathan, according to the statistics, should be doing well in school, but he isn't.

Jonathan's parents had spoken to me about their son and told me how unhappy they were about his situation. They shared with me that he had been retained in first grade because he couldn't read. The retention was suggested by Jonathan's teacher and principal, and they, the parents, hadn't objected because they were told that by repeating the grade, Jonathan would be happier and would do much better. He would have another year to "catch up." The parents were also told that it was better if Jonathan were retained at the beginning of his school career rather than later. It all sounded reasonable, so Jonathan's parents went along.

Well, Jonathan wasn't happier when he repeated first grade, and he wasn't "catching up." Jonathan hated school; his personality was changing, and he felt that he was dumb. He didn't like himself very much.

When Jonathan's parents met with his teacher, Jonathan's teacher said that he was having a great deal of trouble with the reading program the school was using, but it was the only program that the teachers were allowed to use. (The reading program was the same one with which Jonathan had had difficulty the year before.) The teacher told the parents that they shouldn't worry because she was sure that Jonathan would soon adjust to it. Jonathan's parents weren't so sure, so they made an appointment to meet with the school principal. The principal also told them not to worry and that she and her staff knew what was good for Jonathan. They said that after all, they were the professionals. The principal, in addition, said that they were justified in retaining Jonathan because on the group IQ test he had scored in a range that put him in the category of slow learners. The principal said that Jonathan would continue with the same program and the same method of instruction.

Jonathan's parents were confused and bitter. They were worried. The private schools would not accept Jonathan because the school year had begun. Their son was becoming more and more unhappy and he didn't want to go to school. His parents, who had always thought that Jonathan was a bright child, were beginning to wonder whether they were mistaken and that the IQ test score was correct and Jonathan was indeed a slow learner. Jonathan's parents decided to go to outside sources for help. They went to a reading specialist who was qualified to administer individual IQ tests. When the reading specialist met Jonathan, Jonathan blurted out, "I'm glad I'm here because I missed school to come here. I hate school. I'm the biggest one in my class because I was left back. I'm dumb." Ms. Davis (a pseudonym) nodded in a sympathetic way and then engaged Jonathan in some conversation to establish rapport with him. "What do you like to do?" she asked. "I love to go through the magazine *National Geographic,* because I like animals. I go fishing and camping with my father and older brother a lot. I also love sports." Jonathan then proceeded to discuss nocturnal animals and their habitats. Needless to say, Ms. Davis was fascinated. Jonathan did not sound as if he were a slow learner. From listening to his vocabulary and concept development, he appeared to be a highly-able young man.

Ms. Davis decided to give Jonathan some reading assessments that would test his sight vocabulary, his ability to figure out words, and his comprehension ability. When she gave him a list of words in isolation and asked him to state each one, Jonathan picked up the sheet and put it so close to his face that the paper was actually touching his nose. Ms. Davis asked Jonathan if he wore glasses. He said, "No." Throughout the testing session, Jonathan appeared to have great difficulty recognizing words. When Ms. Davis asked him to orally read a very short passage, he was unable to do so. However, when she read aloud to him and asked him questions about the passages, he was able to answer all the questions correctly, including some very hard and involved ones. It was obvious to Ms. Davis that Jonathan had excellent thinking ability. With such good thinking ability, he could not be a slow learner.

Ms. Davis decided to administer an individual IQ test to Jonathan. Her suspicions were realized; Jonathan is a highly able child. He certainly is not "dumb"; the term he applied to himself. A crime had been perpetrated against Jonathan. Who is to blame?

Jonathan's parents love him. They have provided a warm, enriched, and understanding home environment for him. His world has been filled with books, travel, museums, farms, zoos, and adventure. He has an excellent listening and speaking vocabulary. However, something went wrong. What?

First, Jonathan's parents should have noticed from his behavior that he had some kind of eye problem. It seems almost incredible that they were unaware of this. When Ms. Davis asked Jonathan's parents about this, they said that they had been thinking of taking him to an eye doctor because they had noticed that he sat so close to the TV, but so did all his friends. They also claimed that the school nurse had tested Jonathan's eyes and had found no eye problem. When Jonathan, however, was eventually taken to an eye doctor, the doctor found that he had a very severe astigmatism, which would account for Jonathan's difficulty with recognizing words on the printed page. Jonathan had difficulty focusing on words.

Jonathan's parents should have been more questioning when they learned that their child was having problems learning to read. They should not have allowed him to be retained on the basis of a group IQ test; they should have wondered why their bright child was doing so poorly. They should have had more faith in their son and his ability, and they should have requested that he have more extensive testing before he was retained.

The school had given him a group IQ test, which required him to circle words and letters, which he couldn't clearly see. They then used this test to justify his retention. Then the school put Jonathan in a class with the same teacher and gave him the exact same program that didn't work the first time! They were matching the child to the curriculum rather than the curriculum to the child. The school's behavior was reprehensible.

The school should have had Jonathan tested by a child study team and an individual IQ test should have been administered to him by a qualified professional.

It is also a sad commentary on Jonathan's school situation that his teacher didn't recognize that Jonathan showed signs of having an eye problem. In addition, his teacher should have noticed that Jonathan's excellent listening and speaking vocabulary belied his being a slow learner. Jonathan was not merely verbalizing; he knew the meanings of the words.

We could go on and on. Regardless as to who is to blame, Jonathan almost became a first-grade failure. Fortunately for Jonathan, his parents persisted and sought outside help for him; consequently, this story has a happy ending. Unfortunately, the same cannot be said for many other children.

I am sharing this case study with you to raise your consciousness level to the fact that there are many factors that influence a child's ability to read. And one very important factor that is often overlooked because it is so obvious—is vision.

In addition, parents should not allow themselves to be intimidated by school personnel or whomever if they feel that something is just not "right" with their child. Certainly, the more parents know about their child and learning, the more able parents will be to help their child.

I hope what I have written helps you.

Question 53: What is the relationship of reading to school dropouts?

Dear Dr. Rubin,

What is the relationship between reading and school dropouts?

Sincerely,
Curious Parent

Dear Curious Parent,

According to "Years of Promise," a report sponsored by the Carnegie Corporation of New York, students' poor performance is due to their reading problems. If children aren't reading by third grade, they are at risk for becoming dropout candidates.

Question 54: Who are the majority of school dropouts?

Dear Dr. Rubin,

Who are the majority of school dropouts?

> Sincerely,
> Questioning Parent

Dear Questioning Parent,

According to the Carnegie report (sponsored by the Carnegie Corporation of New York), the majority of school dropouts aren't poor. The report states that Americans "must come to terms with the fact that many middle- and upper-income children are failing to thrive intellectually." It was also reported that by fourth grade, most children's school performance is below grade level. The Carnegie report seems to corroborate the National Assessment of Educational Progress reading reports, which find that too many fourth graders are not scoring at the proficient level.

Question 55: Will an army of volunteers help children become good readers?

Dear Dr. Rubin,

Will an army of volunteers help children become good readers?

> Sincerely,
> Involved Parent

Dear Involved Parent,

As laudable as this concept is, what we need more than volunteers are teachers in the early grades who know how to teach children to read and who can nip problems in the bud. Unfortunately, we have many teachers who are lacking these skills through no fault of their own. Many new teachers were trained in schools of education that stressed a whole language philosophy rather than a balanced approach to the teaching of reading.

Consequently, many teachers didn't gain the specific reading skills and strategies they need. And when many of these new teachers enter the classroom, they are often at their wit's end when it comes to teaching reading.

NOTES

© FEARON TEACHER AIDS FE211001

 *Homework*

Question 56: Why does the start of the school year bring stress to numerous parents?

Dear Dr. Rubin,

I used to look forward to the start of school for my children. Today, however, the start of the school year seems to bring with it a time of great stress. I need a reprieve from school and all the homework my daughter brings home. I want my child to get homework. I know it's important, but this is ridiculous. My daughter comes home with so much work that she doesn't have time to do anything else. I also resent that I have to practically teach her the concepts and skills she doesn't seem to get in school. And my feelings are shared by lots of other parents. I know one mother who's working part-time to be able to pay for an after-school learning center to teach her child.

It seems as though the assignments are so involved that without parental intervention, the children would hardly ever finish. Actually, in looking at my daughter's assignments, I'd say that you have to be very educated to be able to help with the assignments. Fortunately, I'm home and not working. But what about the single-parent homes or homes where both parents work full time?

What bothers me is that today children just don't seem to have time to be children. All my friends feel the same as I do. One of my friends who has a son in third grade said that from the moment he gets home from school until almost bedtime, he's doing homework. My friend is concerned about how much work he'll have next year.

She and I laugh a lot when people and especially educators say that now is the time for our children to be reading just for fun. Our children have even had to opt out of playing soccer because they just don't have the time. I feel that my child is losing her childhood. And I'm not alone in how I feel. Practically all the parents I talk to feel the same way. There must be some solution, but I don't know what. We talk to the teachers, so for one or two days, the children have less work, then it starts all over again. Please help.

Sincerely,
Stressed-Out Parent

SECTION V

Dear Stressed-Out Parent,

I'm sorry that your child's homework has caused you so much grief. I feel that the best way to help you is to provide you with a question and answer guide on homework that I have compiled primarily for parents. I hope it helps you and your friends in similar situations.

Question and Answer Guide on Homework

Question 57: What is homework?

ANSWER: Homework is school-related work done at home.

Question 58: How important is homework?

ANSWER: Homework plays an important role in education today. Numerous studies have shown that the investment of significant amounts of time in homework is related to success in school for children at all ability levels. And the 1990 National Assessment of Educational Progress' summary report states that homework gives students experience in following directions, making judgments, working through problems alone, and developing responsibility and self-discipline. This having been said, it is imperative to state that according to a major review of the literature on homework "Researchers do not agree . . . on the advantages and disadvantages of homework as an instructional tool." It is interesting to note that for elementary-school children, the relationship between homework and achievement is "almost zero." The relationship is greater for middle-school students and the highest for high-school students. In other words, the effect on achievement is large in high school but small in the lower grades.

Question 59: Why is homework given?

ANSWER: Time-on-task research strongly suggests that students' active learning time is an essential factor in raising students' achievement. And one inexpensive way to increase learning time is to increase homework assignments. It's not surprising then that homework studies show that homework, under certain conditions, at certain grade levels does improve test scores and grades.

Question 60: How much homework should children be given?

ANSWER: Recently, a concerned parent said that she had heard that her third-grader would be getting a teacher who was known for giving lots of homework. The teacher had told her previous children's parents that she felt that at third grade, children should receive at least one hour of homework every day. The anxious parent was worried because her son was a bright student, but he was very meticulous; consequently, it took him a long time to finish his work. The parent felt that her child would be up half the night doing homework and that it would put stress on her child and the whole family. The parent wanted to know how much homework students should be given.

The question concerning how much homework children should be given may seem simple, but it's an exceedingly complex one because it depends on many factors. Obviously teachers must take into account the grade and maturity level of their students when it comes to homework.

Students will spend different amounts of time on doing homework based on their backgrounds, so absolutes cannot be made concerning how much time students must spend in this area. A National Assessment of Educational Progress report, in relation to homework and reading proficiency, found that on average for 17-year-olds, more homework was beneficial. However, for 13-year-olds there was no difference in effect, and for nine-year-olds more than 2 hours of homework seemed to have a negative effect on their reading proficiency.

Question 61: How much homework should first- to third-graders be given?

ANSWER: Homework is not recommended for children in first grade. Today, however, many teachers are starting to assign homework at the first-grade level. A small amount of homework is fine if it's interesting, related to what the children are doing, and if teachers inform parents how they can help their children. It's, however, absurd to overload children with so much work that they don't have time to read or do anything else.

In first grade, assigned homework should not require more than 15 or 20 minutes a day and it should be child-oriented rather than parent-oriented. It is also important to state that if homework is given in first grade, the school system should have good reasons for its recommendations.

At the third grade, when teachers usually become serious about giving homework, children should be assigned homework for about 30 to 40 minutes. If the children's homework assignments exceed this amount or if third-graders have no homework, parents should discuss this with their children's teacher.

Question 62: Why is homework often referred to as "mindless drudgery"?

ANSWER: Unfortunately, homework has received a "bad rap" because numerous teachers do not have an effective homework policy. They often do not give students meaningful and challenging homework based on their students' developmental levels. They also may not go over the homework. By just piling on homework, teachers do not recognize that students have other activities that vie for their time and attention.

It is important that the positive reports on the relationship of homework to achievement in the upper grades do not become ends unto themselves or even counter-productive. Overburdening children with excessive homework in the hopes of increasing their achievement, or using homework as punishment or busy work, is undesirable and can be harmful and turn off students from school.

Question 63: What is the relationship of homework to the home?

ANSWER: A major purpose of homework is to link the school with the home—not to be a wedge between the two.

Question 64: Should parents help children with homework?

ANSWER: Certainly, parents should oversee their children's homework. But overseeing homework is different from having to teach the concepts that should have been taught in school. Of course, parents may need to explain some concepts at times, but this shouldn't be a regular practice. In other words, parents should help their children when they need assistance, but they shouldn't have to do the assignments for them. If teachers' homework assignments overwhelm parents, this feeling will carry over to their children.

Question 65: What are some specific things that parents can do to help their children?

ANSWER: Parents can provide their children with a place to study or do their homework. This area should be comfortable, convenient, have enough light, and be free from distractions.

Providing a place for children may seem simple enough; however, it can be a problem. There are many children who do not have a room of their own or any special place to do their homework. There are children who live in cramped quarters and those who live in homes that are never free from distractions. There are some who do not have a home. These children need special help and consideration. Parents and the schools should work together to try to provide places where children who do not have a place to study can do their homework.

Parents should also make sure that the place they choose is one where their children will not be disturbed. And very importantly, parents should make sure that they don't plan special exciting events during school nights that will compete with their children's homework.

In addition, parents should help children recognize the importance of planning and how planning can help them make the most efficient use of their time. They can help their young children draw up a plan that includes a rhythm of activities and that spreads out their homework and studying over the week.

Question 66: What is the role of teachers in assigning homework?

ANSWER: When teachers assign homework, the work should be based on the developmental levels of the children, and the children should be given sufficient time to complete home projects. Teachers should ask themselves about the purpose of the assignment, its relevance to class work, and whether it's reasonable. In addition, teachers should clearly explain the assignment and model for their students what they should be doing. And not only should teachers correlate their assignment with the homework students have in other subjects, but they should also take into account that children have other things to do.

Question 67: What recourse do parents have if they are concerned about their children's homework assignments?

ANSWER: Parents should have major input in relation to homework policies. Parents could talk to their children's teachers, the principal and the school board members about their concerns. They also could recommend that the school examine its homework policy. Parents also, through their Parent Teacher Association (PTA), could make certain recommendations concerning homework to the school board. In addition, parents could volunteer to be on a committee to examine the school system's homework policy.

Question 68: What resources are available to help children with their homework?

ANSWER: Some schools provide hotlines for families whereby parents or children can phone to find out not only what an assignment is but also to receive help on doing the assignment. Some schools also provide after-school help for those students who need assistance. Often these after-school programs are staffed by retirees, teachers, and parents.

The Internet also provides special homework help. Parents should recognize that various Internet sites are for-profit and available only if they become members. Many learning centers are also available to help children with homework, but this too can be costly.

Parents, however, shouldn't have to shell out money for the kind of help that should be provided in school. It's just one more burden put upon parents' already overburdened shoulders.

NOTES

 Study Skills

Question 69: What is the relationship between study skills and homework?

Dear Dr. Rubin,

What is the relationship between study skills and homework?

Sincerely,
Concerned Parent

Dear Concerned Parent,

Homework and study skills are closely related. Many students today are weighed down with a lot of homework; consequently, they more than ever need to be good planners and have excellent study skills. Most primary-grade children, however, aren't helped to gain important study skills. When parents notice that it's taking their children an inordinate amount of time to finish their homework, they often attempt to provide them with the necessary study skills or send their children to a learning center to acquire the needed skills.

P.S. I am enclosing for your information a question and answer guide on study skills that you might find useful.

Question and Answer Guide on Study Skills

Question 70: What are good study skills?

ANSWER: Students usually need a set time to study. A regular plan will prevent confusion. In addition, students need to learn early on that distributing their studying over a period of time will help them retain the information over an extended period of time. Another important step in building good study habits concerns the amount of time to spend in studying. This factor will vary from student to student because it depends on the subject and how well students know it.

Consistency is very important. By studying or doing their homework in the same place each time, the children are associating a certain place with studying. As a result, it may take the children less time to adjust and settle down to the task of doing their homework.

Question 71: What kinds of study skills do good students have?

ANSWER: Good students are generally good planners who make effective use of their time. They set short- and long-term goals for themselves and attempt to accomplish these goals by organizing their time realistically; that is, they include time for such essential activities as sleeping, eating, and recreation, as well as study time.

Question 72: What is the school's role in providing study skills?

ANSWER: Numbers of primary-grade teachers feel that their students are too young to receive study skill help and aid in organizing their time better. Many state that they don't have the time to provide study skill help. First grade is not too soon to begin children on the road to acquiring good study skills. It's the school's responsibility to help students acquire good study skills as soon as possible before they develop either poor study habits or erroneous concepts concerning studying. And teachers' time would be well-spent providing students with study skills because knowledge of how to study can help students in all their content areas. Throughout the grades, teachers should help students realize that with good study habits, they could spend less time in studying and learn more. Teachers should also make sure their students understand that even if students think they know something well, students still should spend some time to review the material and go over key concepts.

Question 73: Can children study and listen to music and watch television at the same time?

ANSWER: Note that "free from distractions" is an essential element in studying. Some children claim that they can do homework, listen to music, watch television, and carry on a conversation at the same time. This is definitely not true. Extra demands, such as watching television or listening to music, can take away from the students' primary task. Distractions interfere with concentration. And concentration, which is sustained attention, is essential for studying and doing homework.

Question 74: Does playing music while children are doing homework help them do better?

ANSWER: The concept of using multimedia to enhance children's learning makes sense, however, not when children are studying or concentrating on something else. Playing music while children are studying or while in school taking a test could cause a sensory overload for most of the children. When children, or any individuals, are concentrating, they are tuning out the music because it is interfering with their concentration. Using multimedia doesn't mean that different media should be vying for children's attention. It means that various media should be used to appeal to children's different senses and that the media should be used separately.

Question 75: What is the role of concentration in studying?

ANSWER: Concentration demands a mental set or attitude, a determination that individuals will block everything out except what they are reading, studying, or listening to. Of course, paying attention doesn't guarantee that students will understand what they are reading or listening to; however, concentration is an important first step. Without concentration, there is little hope that students will understand the information or concepts being presented.

Question 76: What can parents do to help their children concentrate better?

ANSWER: Parents can provide a home environment conducive to concentration when their children are studying or doing homework. If a room is too hot or cold, if their children are hungry, if they are tired or sleepy, if the chairs that the children are sitting in are uncomfortable, if the lighting is poor, or if there are auditory or visual distractions, most children will not be able to concentrate.

NOTES

 Sex Education

Question 77: Should there be comprehensive sex education programs for five- to eight-year-old children?

Dear Dr. Rubin,

My school district is considering starting a comprehensive sex education program beginning at kindergarten. My husband and I looked at the program that our school is thinking of initiating and we were aghast at how explicit it is for kindergarten children. Please give us your views concerning sex education for children five to eight years old.

> Sincerely,
> Outraged Parents

Dear Outraged Parents,

A few decades ago, it was considered progressive to have sex education in the sixth grade. And when sex education did take place, it was usually in a restrictive environment. For example, in one school, all the boys left the room so that the girls could stay and learn about "babies." Many educators felt that such an environment would be less embarrassing and that the sixth-grade girls would feel more free to ask questions. Boys were usually exempt from such education because it was reasoned that since boys did not have to worry about menstruation, they didn't need to learn anything about it or its consequences, that is, until high school biology.

Times have changed. In this age of AIDS, teenage pregnancies, and sexual promiscuity among young people, enlightened educators have recognized that waiting for high school biology for both sexes to learn about human sexuality is rather naive.

The problem, however, is that now some educators seem to want to go to the other extreme—these people want comprehensive sex education to begin for children as early as kindergarten. And those individuals who claim that much of the material is not age-appropriate and does not make sense based on what is known about children's growth and development—especially cognitive development—are often called names and branded as fanatics or zealots, even though they are not.

I do not recommend an explicit sex education program for five- to eight-year-olds. Why flood young children's minds with information about sex that they will have difficulty processing? Enclosed for your information is my question and answer guide on sex education for five- to eight-year-olds.

Question and Answer Guide on Sex Education for Five- to Eight-Year-Olds

Question 78: What is the parents' role in determining what sex education programs schools adopt for their five- to eight-year-old children?

ANSWER: Parents must question a sex education program for five- to eight-year-olds, or for that matter, any kind of program that they may feel is detrimental to their children. Even though the state may mandate that schools provide a family-life program for their students, it is up to the school district to determine what is in the best interests of the children in their community. And here is where parental input is imperative.

Today, in many homes, both parents work. Many may not have the time, even if they have the inclination, to find out what is taking place in their children's schools. If educators claim something is age-appropriate, many parents generally will not challenge this point. And for the most part, there is usually no need to do so.

The school is an integral part of the community it serves. And its curriculum is supposed to be based on the needs of the community and cooperatively developed by the efforts of many people, including parents and students. If parents feel that the schools are not serving their children well, they have a right and a duty to become informed about what is taking place.

Question 79: Should parents take time to review their young children's family-life (sex education) program?

ANSWER: Definitely! All parents should take the time to read their children's family-life program. Take, for example, a particular family-life program for kindergarten through third grade that is now in a number of schools. Even though the chart at the beginning of the program suggests some topics, such as "How Babies Begin," for second- to third-graders, it has a special note in the body of the book that states "How Babies Begin, Part One," might be used for kindergarten through first grade. And throughout the program for almost all topics there are activities for kindergarten through third grade.

How many parents feel their second- or third-graders are ready for an X-rated graphic description of the sex act that explicitly explains, in precise detail, how a man and a woman while loving each other produce a baby?

I have no problems with young children learning the anatomically correct names for certain body parts. However, why should kindergartners and first-graders have an activity that asks them to "make a list of healthful foods that a pregnant woman should eat?" In addition, what's the purpose of telling such young children that "sex makes your body feel very good; it tells the other person that you love them very much . . ."? Are we piquing their interest so they will be tempted to try it as soon as possible?

When it comes to sex education, the parents must be involved in determining what is age-appropriate for their children. One good way to make sure this happens is for parents to become actively involved in helping to develop a family-life curriculum that will best suit their children.

Question 80: What are some usual reasons producers of explicit family-life programs give to defend beginning their programs in kindergarten?

ANSWER: Many such people feel that those against their program are naive, that young children know much more than their parents think, and that children are talking about it. They want children to be given the "straight" information when they are young rather than to "spring" it on them later on.

Question 81: How should parents answer young children's questions about sex?

ANSWER: Young children usually are talking about their "private parts." And they will often ask why members of the opposite sex have different private parts. When children ask this question, they usually do not want a detailed, belabored explanation. They want and need a simple, truthful answer that parents can generally supply.

Young children are also talking about babies and where they come from; however, this does not mean that they want or need a detailed, graphic explanation about intercourse. Yes, we should give them the correct terms for their genitalia, but that is light years away from discussing intercourse. Also, giving correct terminology does not also mean that teachers should encourage young children to draw these private parts as some family-life activities advocate.

Question 82: Do young children have the cognitive ability to process sex information?

ANSWER: Most early-primary grade children usually do not have the cognitive ability to comprehend complex concepts such as intercourse. This concept will probably confuse most of them and frighten many of them.

Question 83: What kind of sex information should be given to young children?

ANSWER: The information presented must be based on what we know about children's social, emotional, and cognitive development. Early-primary grade children gain information from firsthand and concrete experiences. It's ludicrous to assume that teachers would therefore help children understand the concept of intercourse using anatomically correct male and female dolls.

Question 84: What are some questions that schools should be prepared to answer concerning their family-life program for young children?

ANSWER: How much information should be given? How explicit should it be? At what ages should the information be given? How should it be presented? Who in the school system should present the information?

Question 85: What can schools do to help parents talk to their children about sex?

ANSWER: It's a good idea for schools to make available sex education material on topics such as intercourse and conception to help those parents who wish to discuss these topics with their young children. That is the parents' or caregivers' prerogative.

NOTES

Other School-Related Topics

Question 86: How important is the first-grade teacher?

Dear Dr. Rubin,

My child will be entering first grade next year. How important is her first-grade teacher? Also, what can I do to make sure she gets a good first-grade teacher?

> Sincerely,
> Anxious Parent

Dear Anxious Parent,

You are wise to be concerned about having a good first-grade teacher for your child because the first grade is an exceptionally critical one for all children—it is usually when formal reading and writing begin. And children's subsequent success in school often hinges on their success or failure in first grade.

Today, a great deal of attention is being paid to children's preschool years and their importance in intellectual and language development. This is good! We cannot, however, use the importance of the preschool years as an excuse for not helping children when they do come to school. Rather than blame social and economic factors over which we have little control, we should be trying to do more where we can—in the schools.

Solutions ranging from recertification to the extended school year to vouchers and so on have been put forth as ways to enhance students' achievement. These proposals, however, do not hit at the heart of the problem. What is needed are more teachers qualified to teach reading, especially in the first grade. A poor teacher can negatively influence children's feelings toward learning, and this attitude can stay with the children all through their school years.

The first grade should have the most qualified and experienced teachers. No primary-grade teacher should be allowed in the classroom without knowledge of developmental reading, diagnostic techniques, instructional strategies, child growth and development, and the sensitivity necessary to help children.

Parents should visit various first-grade classes to observe what teachers are doing. What follows is a portrait of a first-grade teacher that should help guide you in recognizing the kinds of traits a good first-grade teacher should have.

Ms. Ramirez's love of children, reading, and teaching are evident when you enter her room. You are immediately taken by the smiling faces of children busily engaged in various activities. Some of the children are standing by bookshelves leafing through books; a few are looking at a big book together. Some are working at their desks; some are working with Ms. Ramirez, and two are working on the computer. In another corner, there are two children who are writing a story together that they will share later with the class. In yet another part of the room, there are three children working with puppets preparing to present a skit to the class.

Ms. Ramirez has a wonderful emotional environment in her classroom. Children feel free to be risk-takers. Of course, this environment did not just happen. Ms. Ramirez is a master teacher. She uses her background in child growth and development and learning theory to develop a classroom environment where children feel good about themselves and want to learn.

She is aware of the children in her classroom and respects their individual differences by preparing lessons based on their needs and interests. She uses multiple criteria for grouping and employs flexible grouping in her class; that is, she works with the whole class, individual children, large groups, small groups, ad-hoc groups, and so forth. And very importantly, students can move from one group to another. In addition, children, from time to time, are involved in cooperative or collaborative groups, whereby the children work together toward a common goal.

Ms. Ramirez believes in a balanced approach to the teaching of reading. She integrates the language arts, which are listening, speaking, reading, writing, and viewing; draws from many different sources; and uses a variety of materials in teaching. She uses different types of print material and stories, as well as basal readers; presents a sequential development of skills, which she relates to what children are learning; and gives her students many opportunities to read and write.

In addition, she uses various methods of instruction, especially modeling. She believes that teachers should be facilitators and guides, but they must also have strategies at their fingertips to directly help students gain understanding. Ms. Ramirez knows when to do what and how. She is especially adept at knowing when to intervene to enhance her students' understanding.

Ms. Ramirez treats each child with dignity and respect. She is aware of the latest research on gender differences and makes sure that she challenges and encourages children of both sexes. She is always on the lookout for children who tease others or who make other children feel insecure. She meets with parents and solicits their help in working with the children. She keeps parents informed of what their children are doing with a monthly newsletter she sends to them. With the newsletter, she includes a short narrative that tells each parent something special about each child.

Is it any wonder that parents wish they could clone Ms. Ramirez so that all first-graders could have her as their teacher?

I hope my letter has helped you.

Question 87: Should children be retained in school?

Dear Dr. Rubin,

Help! Our son is having a terrible time in school. He has repeated first grade because the school said that it would be best since he was having difficultly learning to read. We went along with the school's advice. Now we're not sure we did the right thing. Our son hates school. He refuses to go. We just don't know what to do.

We should tell you that this year in school is literally a repeat of last year. He has the same teacher and he also is doing the same work. We are trying to help him at home, but he is rebelling. We don't understand why the teacher is doing the same things with our son that didn't work before.

Needless to say, we are extremely frustrated. Also, we have noticed that our son's friends who had been in his first-grade class and are now in second grade don't seem to be reading that much better than our son. We're now wondering whether we did the right thing to allow our child to be retained.

Our son has always been a delight. He is a precious child, but his personality is changing. Any advice or help you can give us will be gratefully appreciated.

Sincerely,
Frustrated Parents

Dear Frustrated Parents,

You have every right to wonder about your decision. First of all, if the child didn't do well in the same program before, the teacher should use different methods to help him gain the skills and strategies he needs to be able to read. And your confusion concerning retention versus promotion is understandable because so many in the educational community are also confused about this issue.

A number of years ago, there was an amazing headline that read, "No more Failures in School!" This eye-catching headline was the result of numerous studies which suggested that children, on average, who weren't promoted not only didn't fare any better than those in the same situation who were promoted, but they actually did worse.

A problem with retention is that even though children may not do well academically, they are still developing socially, emotionally, and physically. Therefore, children who repeat a grade usually have difficulty making acceptable social adjustments; they generally lack self-confidence, and many often view their retention as punishment. All these factors can translate into more aggressive and antagonistic behavior on the part of the non-promoted children, which may cause many disruptions in class. And an especially disturbing problem is that many students who repeat a grade are subjected to the exact same program in which they didn't do well the year before, even if they don't have the same teacher.

On the other hand, children who are promoted who haven't attained the skills they need to enter the next grade will usually have difficulties also. It appears that these children often suffer from lack of self-confidence; they are generally maladjusted and usually have other problems. Obviously the problems of retention and social promotion, whereby students are promoted based on chronological age rather than academic achievement, have certain advantages and disadvantages.

Having said this, it is important to state that a blanket social promotion policy shouldn't be initiated. It makes sense that the individual differences of the students must be taken into account when determining whether to promote or retain them. And the parents are key people in helping the school system make this very difficult decision.

In addition, and very, very importantly, if children are retained, the school system must make sure that these children are properly diagnosed and given the special help they need. They certainly should not have to repeat the same program that previously hadn't worked for them!

Good Luck!

Question 88: What should be done for a child who has been retained a grade level?

Dear Dr. Rubin,

My daughter has repeated first grade, but we do not notice any improvement in her reading. All we know is that she is very unhappy. We were told last year that by repeating the first grade she would have another year to catch up.

Our daughter is in a school that uses the same program for every child. And the teacher said that it is the only program the school is allowed to use. When we met with her teacher last year, we were told that they were justified in retaining our daughter because she scored very low on both the group achievement and IQ test that they had given her.

The assessments are confusing to us because our daughter has an excellent vocabulary. When she talks to us she seems to have a good grasp of what she's talking about. Also, when we read stories aloud to her, she can repeat the story to us almost verbatim and she has no problems answering questions about the story.

Even though we were confused, we went along with the school's recommendation because, after all, they are the professionals. We realize now that we might have been too trusting. What would you suggest we do now?

Sincerely yours,
Bitter Parents

Dear Bitter Parents,

Was your child tested by a child study team before she was retained? I strongly suggest you have your child tested by outside reading professionals who are well versed in diagnosing reading problems. Such persons would look at the possibility of both educative and noneducative factors that could be interfering with your child's being able to read.

Because you claim that your child has good comprehension when you read aloud to her, she may have some perceptual problems, such as hearing and sight. I would recommend that your child have her hearing and eyesight tested. It could be that she has a severe astigmatism or that she is farsighted. These eye defects could interfere with the ability to decode words on the printed page. It could also be that she hasn't been presented with the word recognition skills she needs to decode words from the printed page. Obviously, I can only hypothesize what the problem or problems may be.

I strongly suggest that you speak to your daughter's teacher and voice your feelings. If you do not receive any satisfaction, then you should speak to the principal. Make sure you receive a plan that will tell you what they expect your daughter to be doing.

I wish you luck.

Question 89: Is learning in a single-gender environment better?

Dear Dr. Rubin,

Many of my friends feel that their children will learn more if they are in a single-gender environment. What do you think?

Sincerely,
Confused Parent

Dear Confused Parent,

There's a lot of conflicting information concerning gender differences, which is difficult to sort out. And those assuming that the move to single-gender classes or any other solution will cure educational ills are in for a rude awakening. Single-gender classes should be an option for those who feel more comfortable in classes without the opposite sex. The world-at-large, however, is coed, so it seems that the sooner the two sexes learn to get along with one another in school, the better they will get along in the workplace.

P.S. I am including a question and answer guide on single-gender learning that I hope will help answer some other questions you may have.

Question and Answer Guide on Single-Gender Learning

Question 90: What are some noneducative gender differences?

ANSWER: For a while it was considered almost heresy to state that gender differences exist. It, however, isn't difficult to recognize that boys and girls are different, even though during the unisex period, physical differences between the genders may not have been too obvious at first glance.

Despite changes in females' lifestyles, actuary tables still show there's a greater death and disease rate among males than females. And now a research report claims that for the first time, there may be slightly fewer male than female births. Bad news reports about the well-being of males isn't new. It has been suggested that females have a biological precocity evident from birth onward and that the skeletal development of girls is superior to boys at birth, and this physical superiority continues until maturity. By sixth grade, on average, girls are about two years more mature than boys. It has also been hypothesized that males' metabolism may contribute to their having a greater incidence of disease than females.

Question 91: What are some educative gender differences?

ANSWER: When children begin school, boys, on average, aren't as mature as some girls of the same age. And although studies reveal no significant differences between males and females in general intelligence, there appear to be some differences in specific aptitudes. For example, it consistently has been found that girls usually surpass boys in verbal ability. However, females don't have larger meaning vocabularies than males. And males, on average, do better in math and science. Studies, such as the National Assessment of Educational Progress (NAEP), continue to report that boys do not, on average, do as well as girls when it comes to writing and language skills, even though males appear to be narrowing the gap in verbal areas. And even though the NAEP science report indicates that males, on average, surpass females in science, girls' math and science scores have greatly improved and have narrowed the gap between the two sexes. It has been suggested that gender bias may play a role in males' superiority in quantitative reasoning and science. Gender bias charges on tests such as the SAT college-entrance exam have been going on for a long time. To offset these accusations, the Educational Testing Service (ETS), producers of the SAT, did a four-year study to determine if such bias exists. The study, which concluded in 1997, found more similarities than differences in girls' and boys' performances. On the ETS study, gender differences weren't influenced by additional testing time, guessing-type questions, or open-ended questions. However, on a recent NAEP science exam, eighth-grade girls did as well as the boys. And it was hypothesized that this may be due to the open-ended questions that were included. The gender battle concerning the SAT still rages.

In 1992, researchers at the Wellesley College Center for Research on Women suggested that teachers are biased in favor of boys. The investigators claimed that girls are short-changed in school settings. They stated that "the educational system is not meeting girls' needs. Girl and boys enter school roughly equal in measured ability . . . . Twelve years later, girls have fallen behind their classmates in key areas, such as higher-level mathematics and measures of self-esteem." Some researchers skeptical of the Wellesley research, found fault with the data. And some questioned the findings that schools favor boys and feel that the opposite is true, especially in the elementary grades, since females, on average, receive higher grades than males. However, the Wellesley research, combined with the consistently lower female scores in math and science on the SATs and in the upper grades on the NAEP reports, convinced many that something drastic had to be done to reverse the trend. The idea they latched onto is sex-segregated schools. Soon a proliferation of these schools dotted the country. A recent study by the American Association of Women (AAUW) reported that segregated schools are popular, they seem to raise girls' self-esteem and help spark their interest in math and science. However, the AAUW study found no evidence that single-sex schools prepare students better academically or that boys or girls achieve better in such environments. Interestingly, in the single-sex private schools where students achieved higher than their counterparts in coed classes, the study suggests that it wasn't gender that was the reason for the difference but rather more stringent courses, tighter discipline, smaller class size, and very highly qualified instructors.

Question 92: What is the purpose of within-class ability grouping?

Dear Dr. Rubin,

My daughter is in a second-grade class in a school district where the superintendent will not allow any grouping within classrooms. He claims that it's undemocratic. My daughter is bored silly because the teacher teaches the whole class everything together. There are a number of children in the class who can't read. There are others, like my daughter, who can read very well. The teacher claims that she would like to group the children, but she can't because of the superintendent's philosophy. How do you feel about what is taking place in my daughter's second-grade class? Do you agree with the superintendent?

Sincerely,
Frustrated Parent

Dear Frustrated Parent,

I believe in within-class flexible grouping. This means that children can move from group to group based on need. Within-class grouping makes sense to me. Good teachers determine students' strengths and weaknesses and then develop a program based on their needs. If teachers find that a number of students have similar kinds of difficulties, they could work with them in a group.

It is disturbing that there are still schools that practice extremism. But it is even more disturbing that educators politicize the educational process. To say that it's undemocratic to group children according to their developmental needs implies that "leveling" is part of the democratic process. It also implies that teachers are supposed to ignore the individual differences of their students.

Today, most elementary classrooms are heterogeneously grouped, that is, children at approximately the same chronological age with different ability and achievement levels are found in the same classroom. And, today, with inclusion, the mental age span within a regular education classroom is greater than it has ever been. The point is that it doesn't make sense to teach a subject such as reading at a single level to a class of children who are at different developmental levels.

Since it is not practical or even possible to provide a completely different individualized program for students in each specific area, it helps to group children according to their needs. Grouping students with other students who require similar help is logical and makes good use of scarce teacher time.

Question 93: What should parents know about the sequence of writing skills in children?

Dear Dr. Rubin,

What should parents know about the sequence of writing skills in children? I want to know if I'm doing everything I can for my preschooler.

Sincerely,
Concerned Parent

Dear Concerned Parent,

When children of about two and one-half first put pencil or crayon to paper, they are entering the initial stage of writing. The desire to convey something of one's own on paper is a necessary first step.

Parents should create a stimulating environment for preschoolers so that children can scribble and express themselves. After preschoolers have committed themselves on paper, they should be encouraged to tell about what they have drawn or "written." A number of preschoolers try their skills at writing stories, even though they do not have specific hand motor control. Showing enthusiasm about the child's endeavors will reinforce continuance.

Also, parents should be good role models for their children. Parents who write will be more prone to have children who write. If parents react negatively to writing letters or "thank-you" notes, this will also carry over to their children.

Children will usually remain in the scribble stage until they master control of specific muscles. Three-year-olds are often able to draw circles, showing that they are gaining control of specific hand muscles. By age five, many can construct other geometric figures, such as squares, which require more precision.

Once the child can make figures, such as circles, squares, triangles, and variations of these, his or her written expression takes on a "picture form." Kindergarten children may use these figures to "write a story." Some kindergarten children who have the necessary hand coordination and mental ability are able to construct letters or words. Some can print their names and write a story about themselves or their families.

Question 94: Why are some schools mandating uniforms for their students?

Dear Dr. Rubin,

Almost every morning my family is in an uproar. And believe it or not, it's all about what our daughters should wear to school. We're leaning more and more to the idea of some form of uniforms to avoid this insanity about clothes. And please don't tell us that we should choose the school outfits the night before—we've done that. The only thing that happens is that we have the "craziness" at night. Also, a group of parents are thinking of bringing up the question about having a dress code for our school. Could you please give us some information about what is taking place in schools across the country in relation to uniforms?

> Sincerely,
> Parents at Wit's End

Dear Parents at Wit's End,

Many parents are used to hearing comments such as the following from their children: "I don't know what to wear to school tomorrow." "Everyone will laugh at me if I wear this outfit." "I have nothing to wear."

Most private and parochial schools require their students to wear some type of uniform. School officials claim it prevents peer pressure from dictating certain labels and seems to instill a sense of pride in the school—it promotes a sense of cohesion. Numerous public schools have also adopted some kind of dress code regarding the wearing of uniforms ranging from very flexible, voluntary policies to mandatory ones.

Recently, a parent told me that she couldn't believe that she would be so happy that her child goes to a school where uniforms are compulsory. "It makes life so easy!" she exclaimed. "When I went to public school years ago," she continued, "if anyone even suggested that you wear some sort of uniform, there would have been a rebellion! My friends and I liked to express ourselves and didn't want anyone to dictate to us what we could wear. We looked upon schools that required uniforms as rigid and dictatorial."

The parent then said, "What a waste of time! My friends and I used to spend hours shopping for clothes and at night we would spend a long time trying to decide what to wear. At that time we were more concerned with the statement we were making in relation to our clothes than in concentrating on our school work. I also remember how upset I was if I couldn't get the latest styles and if my parents couldn't afford to get me some of the designer labels that other girls had."

Another parent whose child is a second-grader seemed to voice the same sentiments. She said she likes her daughter's school's dress code because it's flexible enough so that there's still room for students to express their individuality, yet it helps set certain limits. Also, on certain days, students can wear whatever they want.

Uniforms will not make students do better, turn poor teachers into good ones, or enhance an inferior curriculum. They will not provide more parental involvement or give students the kind of education they should be getting. And a dress code will not help instill the kinds of values we would like into students who are "ripping off" and terrorizing other students for their designer-label clothes, which can be a problem in some schools.

A uniform dress code, might take students' minds off what they are going to wear and get them to concentrate more on their school work. It could even increase attendance among those students who were embarrassed or felt ostracized because they didn't have the kind of outfits that other more affluent students had. And it might help students not only take more pride in their appearance but also give them a sense of belonging to a group.

For a uniform policy to work in public schools, it should be a flexible one where students can mix and match from a variety of outfits and colors. And very importantly, parents and students must be involved in the decision-making process.

I know this is a long reply to your letter, but the dress code problem is not an easy one to solve. I hope my letter helps you and your school decide on a policy that is best for you and your children.

Question 95: What is the role of teachers in helping children fit in socially in class?

Dear Dr. Rubin,

We just moved to a new city, so our third-grader is going to a new school. We waited to move until the school year was over, so we wouldn't disrupt Brian's schooling. We also thought it would be easier for him to make friends if he started fresh at the beginning of the school year. How wrong we were. Our son is miserable because he is being ignored by his peers. Our child used to love school, but now he hates it. He uses any excuse he can to stay home. We spoke to our son's teacher about the situation, but she claims that she doesn't believe in interfering. When I visited Brian's class, I noticed that Brian was sitting at a desk by himself on the outskirts around the cluster of other desks. The other children were sitting in clusters of four. I asked the teacher about her seating arrangement and, in particular, why my son was sitting by himself, away from the other pupils.

The teacher told me that she had asked her students to write the names of children they would like to sit next to on a school trip. Next, she made a chart of their responses (sociogram) and seated them accordingly. Since nobody chose my son, the teacher said that she seated him by himself because he's an isolate.

It seems to me that something is terribly wrong here. Please tell us the role of the teacher in a situation such as ours. Also, please explain what a sociogram is because the teacher mentioned that she used this to seat Brian where he is sitting. It doesn't make sense to us.

Sincerely,
Distraught Parents

Dear Distraught Parents,

I can understand why you are upset. I agree that what your son's teacher has done doesn't make sense. The teacher's ridiculous and misguided use of the sociogram aptly illustrates how "a little learning is a dangerous thing."

Even though parents, as children's first teachers, play an extremely important role in helping children embrace the tenet that all individuals are worthy of dignity and respect, children's teachers also have an essential role in nurturing this basic tenet. Teachers are responsible for establishing a healthy, positive emotional environment in their classrooms where children don't feel threatened, and where they aren't anxious or fearful.

A nonthreatening atmosphere is set by the teachers' acceptance, respect, and understanding of each child in their classes. Teachers who are consistent, fair, stable, emotionally mature, perceptive, and sensitive to the varying personalities in their midst will help provide an effective classroom learning environment. Children who gain recognition and approval in the classroom for their positive attitudes and treatment of others are often more ready to give recognition and approval to others.

A positive classroom social environment, where students are accepting of others, is strongly dependent on the presence of a positive emotional environment. Teachers who show by their behavior that they respect all students and who try to help new students are setting good examples for their pupils because students often emulate teachers' behavior. And students who are accepted by their peers and teachers are more likely to look forward to coming to school.

Teachers can learn about the social relations of the students in their classes by means of a sociogram, a map or chart showing the interrelationships of the children in the classroom. The sociogram identifies those who are "stars," chosen the most by others, and "isolates," not chosen by anyone. (Perceptive teachers probably already know who their "stars" and "isolates" are.)

Teachers are supposed to use the results of tools such as sociograms to help them improve their classes' emotional and social classroom environment. And teachers are supposed to try to help children who are "isolates" rather than seat them according to the sociograms' results.

Teachers cannot accurately determine who will be friends with whom in school and certainly not out of school—nor is this their responsibility. Also, teachers cannot change "isolates" into "stars." Many ingredients, such as the students' personality, go into making children "stars." Teachers should, however, be aware of the social interactions among the students in their classes and use this information to help their newcomers become assimilated in their classes and consequently help lessen their chances of becoming "isolates."

Perceptive teachers should also provide numerous opportunities for students to gain some insight into their behavior. For example, teachers can read aloud stories that deal with the problems new students might have. Before reading aloud the ending, teachers could have their students use creative problem solving to figure out how to make new students feel at home. They could also have students write their own story endings. Then students could compare their endings to the story's ending and determine which they like better and why.

The bottom line is that good teachers do not create or perpetuate "isolates" in their classrooms—they help to integrate all students into the activities within their classrooms.

I would first speak again to Brian's teacher about your concerns. If you are still dissatisfied with the teacher's response, I would speak to the principal. It might be that you could request that your child be moved to another class. Before doing this, however, I would ask permission to observe the other third-grade class or classes. In addition, I would encourage Brian to invite a child after school to come to your house to play with him. I would also speak to the parents of some of the children in Brian's class and see if you can set a play date for Brian with another child after school. I would probably only invite one child at a time because if there are three or more children, Brian, being the new child, might find himself left out.

I hope that my information helps you.

Question 96: What can be done to make parent-teacher conferences effective for both parents and teachers?

Dear Dr. Rubin,

I feel so insecure when I meet with my child's teacher. Can you give me some pointers on how to get the most from the parent-teacher conference? I really would appreciate it.

Sincerely,
Appreciative Parent

Dear Appreciative Parent,

In some schools, the only parent-teacher involvement is through the parent-teacher conference. I hope this is not so in your situation. The conference is an excellent opportunity for parents and teachers to learn to feel more comfortable with one another, as well as exchange information. It's also a good way for parents to learn how their child is doing.

For the conference to work, there must be an exchange of ideas. Both the parent and teacher must have positive attitudes. It's a good idea for parents to give the teacher some insight to their child that only they would know. They should also come equipped with some general and specific questions that they would like answered.

Question 97: When should parent-teacher conferences take place?

Dear Dr. Rubin,

When should parent-teacher conferences take place?

Sincerely,
Interested Parent

Dear Interested Parent,

Parent-teacher conferences need not take place only during the reporting period. Whenever a need for a conference arises is the right time to call for one. It's also a good idea to meet with the teacher before you suspect that a problem exists. A continuous exchange of ideas in an informal way helps make for good, friendly relations and helps parents stay abreast of what their children are doing.

NOTES

 *Allowance*

Question 98: Should young children receive an allowance?

Dear Dr. Rubin,

Practically all the children in my daughter's second-grade class receive an allowance. My husband and I are confused about this. We don't believe in giving an allowance because it somehow seems so crass. Our child is very well taken care of and receives everything that she needs. Are we wrong in not giving her an allowance?

> Sincerely,
> Confused Parents

Dear Confused Parents,

There is no right or wrong answer in relation to allowance. You must do what feels right for you and your family and not worry about what others are doing. I am enclosing a question and answer guide on allowance that you might find informative. I feel that it will probably answer many of your questions.

Question and Answer Guide on Allowance

Question 99: How do you define allowance for children?

ANSWER: Some define it as any money a child receives to obtain necessities, such as lunch and carfare. Others call it monies children get to use beyond necessities, that is, discretionary funds to be used in any way they wish. And still others define "allowance" to mean receiving money for performing certain chores. There are probably many more varieties of allowance arrangements that parents and their children work out together.

Question 100: What should parents of young children know about allowance?

Before answering this question, here are some statements on allowance. Answer "yes" or "no" to each one.

Allowance	Yes	No
1. Children who receive allowances do better in math than those who don't.		
2. Children beginning at four or five years of age should be given an allowance.		
3. Parents who give allowances to their children should set limits on how the allowances should be spent.		
4. Children who don't receive allowances should be expected to perform certain chores in their home as citizens in a family.		
5. Children who receive allowances should get paid extra for every chore they do.		

ANSWER: If you were to compare your answers with others, you probably would find that most people feel it's good to give children an allowance and that the earlier children learn about money, the better money managers they will be as adults. These are, however, only opinions. Miriam Sherman, a clinical psychiatrist, doesn't agree with those who believe four- and five-year-olds should receive an allowance. She feels that this practice isn't in accord with the developmental aspects of what we know about children's understanding of numbers and money concepts. She also doesn't buy into the theory that the earlier children receive an allowance, the better money managers they will be as adults. And she looks askance at those who believe that making young children become part of "family financial decision-making" will help them become more altruistic and defer their needs for others.

Actually, few studies deal with allowance. The results of some of these may surprise people. For example, Sherman discusses one study in which an investigator found that money earned and money given to children by their parents were equally prized. Children, however, who worked for money claimed they were proud to be able to hold a job or perform some tasks for which they were paid by others who weren't family members. Sherman also mentions that no previous study has shown a relationship between children's being adept at money handling and their becoming either a bank president or an embezzler.

Other studies reveal some interesting findings. For example, one investigator suggests that those who earn money differ in handling money, especially in relation to saving, than those who don't earn money. However, the same study didn't find any significant differences in money handling practices between those who received an allowance and those who didn't. A study dealing with adolescents found that at the time of the investigation, about 60 percent of the students received an allowance. There was no evidence, however, that the students regarded the allowance as an educational opportunity in money management. Those in the study looked upon an allowance as an entitlement for basic support or as earned income.

I agree with Sherman that the topic of allowance is filled with contradictory advice and opinions—there are no definitive rights or wrongs. Parents must be wary about those who dogmatically present information as if it were fact. For example, recently a reporter on an evening news show had a segment on allowances and showed how one family dealt with the issue by paying their children for helping out. The reporter then asked someone from a reputable financial publication when an allowance should be given to children. The publication representative who strongly supports giving children allowances to help them become more financially astute feels that parents could begin giving children an allowance beginning at six years of age.

I fear that parents listening to such advice by a person from a well-known financial magazine would probably give it a great amount of credence, even though the studies and knowledge about children's cognitive development do not appear to support the advice.

It seems that money management, like other tasks, is a complicated undertaking that involves many variables, not least of which are personality and emotional factors, as well as other individual differences. And whether or not to give an allowance probably depends more on the parents and what they feel comfortable with, regardless of their economic situations, than anything else.

NOTES

 Early Childhood Parent and Child Activities

Dear Dr. Rubin,

What are some fun, educational activities that I can do with my preschooler?

Sincerely,
Wondering Parent

Dear Wondering Parent,

I am sending you some Early Childhood Parent and Child Activities that you can do with your child. I hope you find them helpful.

This section provides enjoyable educational activities that parents and children can do together.

AUDITORY DISCRIMINATION

In order for your child to be able to work with phonics, he or she must be able to distinguish between and among various kinds of sounds. Children go from being able to discriminate between and among general sounds in the world around them to speech sounds.

Auditory Discrimination Activities for Everyday Sounds

1. Have children listen to sounds around them and state the sounds they hear.

2. Have child close his or her eyes, while you make different sounds, such as using the can opener, opening a drawer, turning on a light, running water, and so forth. Have child identify the sounds.

3. Read a story that contains various sounds (see Question 24 on page 28 for book suggestions). Tell your child to listen carefully because he or she will help to tell the story when it is read the next time. In the second reading, have the child fill in the correct sound that is indicated by the story line and pictures.

4. Ask your child which sounds he or she finds pleasant. Why? Also, find out which sounds bother your child. Again, try to find out why.

Auditory Discrimination Activities for Initial Consonant Sounds

Present your child with three words. Two have similar initial consonant sounds, and one has a different initial consonant sound. Have your child state the two words that have the same beginning consonant sound.

First model the activity for your child, that is, state aloud exactly the steps you go through to figure out the answer. Say the following:

"Listen carefully. I will say three words. The words are *can, took,* and *book*. Which word begins like *baby* and *ball*? Before we begin, let me show you what I do."

Say: "Let me see. I need to choose the one word that begins like *baby* and *ball*."

"I will show you what I do. *Ball* and *baby* begin with a *buh* sound. *Can* and *took* do not begin with a *buh* sound. The word that begins like *baby* and *ball* is *book*."

After you are sure your child understands the concept, present a list of words such as the following to your child.

Target Word

book	cake	fox	box
can	hat	sank	cook
took	call	tank	ball

There are many variations of this activity that you could present to your child based on his or her developmental level.

You could present your child with three words and have him or her choose the two words that begin with the same initial sound. (It's a good idea to first model for your child what to do.) Here are some examples of words you can use with your child:

dog	cat	can
big	sit	ball
tall	Dan	tip
fan	man	fat

You could present your child first with a target word and then with a group of three words. The child has to choose all the words that start like the target word. The difference is that there may be a group of words that has no words that begin like the target word. (Again, first model for your child what to do.) Here are some examples that you can use:

Target Word

fan	sit	man	can
farm	cow	bear	fit
girl	drum	letter	go
pig	big	pat	pan

Auditory Discrimination Activities for Final Consonant Sounds

Present activities to children similar to initial consonant sounds, except that these are for final consonant sounds. Remember, tell your child to listen carefully because you are going to state a word and then he or she has to give you the word or words that have the same ending sound. You may have to repeat the directions a few times for your child. You may also have to give your child a few examples rather than just one. It's a good idea to start with fewer words and then, based on the developmental level of your child, gradually increase the number. It is also better to start with just one word that has the same ending sound. Note, too, that you might want to include words that have no similar final consonant sounds. If you do such an activity, make sure you tell your child that there are some that have no words that end like the word you say.

Here are some target words and others you could use for final consonant sounds:

Target Word

pit	bat	pig	
can	sit	pan	
book	ball	back	
sad	cat	pit	bed
tool	cook	doll	ball
rug	pan	ball	rat (none)

Auditory Discrimination Sentence Fun

State a sentence that repeats the initial sound at the beginning of almost every word. Invite your child to add a word to the sentence that has the same beginning sound as most of the other words. The number of words you use in a sentence will depend on the developmental level of your child. Example: Ben buys a bat. (A child could say: Ben buys a bat and ball.)

You could also have your child make up a sentence that has the same initial sound in almost all the words. It's a good idea to have your child do this based on the initial sound of his or her name.

I Spy: An Auditory Discrimination Game

This game correlates children's observational ability with their ability to match similar sounds.

You can initiate this game, and then have your child be the leader. Say: "I spy something in this room that begins like the word *dog*. What is it?" Your child must give something in the room that begins like *dog*. Again, based on his or her developmental level, you could have the child put the word he or she "spied" into a sentence. (To make this activity even more challenging, you could do this with final consonant sounds.)

Categories and Initial Sounds

This game correlates children's ability to classify and to match sounds.

You can initiate this game, and then have your child be the leader. Say: "I am thinking of a color that begins like the word *round*. What is it?" (red) If your child gives the correct answer, he or she can try to make up a riddle. If this is too difficult for your child, you can continue by giving him or her some of the following:

I am thinking of a girl whose name begins like *Kim*.

I am thinking of a boy whose name begins like *Ben*.

I am thinking of a fruit that begins like *pot*. (pear, plum)

I am thinking of a fruit that begins like *Ben*. (banana)

I am thinking of a pet that begins like *can*. (cat)

I am thinking of a wild animal that begins like *fan*. (fox)

I am thinking of a vegetable that begins like *Bob*. (bean)

I am thinking of something you can write with that begins like *park*. (pen, pencil)

I am thinking of something you wear on your hands when it is cold outside that begins like *mother*. (mittens)

I am thinking of something you wear on your head that begins like *house*. (hat)

Auditory Discrimination for Rhyming Words

1. Read books to children that have rhymes. The Mother Goose books are excellent and so are many of the Dr. Seuss books, such as *The Cat in the Hat* (Random House).

   When you are reading a story that has rhyming words, it's a good idea to have your child try to state what he or she thinks the rhyming word is.

2. Before presenting children with rhyming exercises, make sure children understand the concept. You may have to present your children with more than one example to help them gain this concept. Some children may confuse the same beginning sound with rhyming words, whereas some may give similar rhyming words for beginning initial sounds.

   State a target word. Ask your child to give you a word that rhymes with the first word you say. (Make sure you model what the child is supposed to do before you begin.) Here are some examples:

   Target Word

pan	pit	can
book	took	bank
sit	sat	fit
car	far	can
big	pig	pit
mat	man	sat
wet	bet	win

   Say three words to your child, two of which rhyme. Ask him or her to give you the two words that rhyme. (Again, make sure you model this for your child.)

   Examples:

man	can	mat
tall	book	ball
cake	book	bake
rag	bug	bag
dog	rug	bug
bake	book	look

CONCENTRATION ACTIVITIES

Unless children are able to concentrate, they will not be able to succeed in any task they undertake. Here are some enjoyable activities that you can do at home that can help your child improve his or her concentration, that is, sustained attention.

The Digit-Span Concentration Activity

This activity deals with numbers. The idea is to help your child to increase his or her digit span—how many digits or words your child can grasp at one time. This activity can be repeated at different times during the week over a period of time. The following scale should help in determining how well your children are doing:

On the average, two-and-one-half-year-olds are able to repeat two digits in order, and three-year-olds are able to repeat three digits in order. Children from about the age of four-and-one-half to about seven years of age are able to repeat four digits in order. Seven- to ten-year-olds are usually able to repeat five digits in order. Ten- to fourteen-year-olds are usually able to repeat six digits in order. Fourteen-year-olds to more able adults usually can repeat seven, eight, and nine digits in order. (Digits refer to numbers. One-syllable words may be substituted for digits.)

When you say the digits to your child, you should say them approximately one second apart and not emphasize one number over another.

Say to your child: "Listen carefully. Say the numbers exactly and in the same order as I do. Do not say anything until after I have finished saying all the numbers. Let me show you what I mean. Here are three numbers—7, 1, 4.
Now I will say them 7, 1, 4. Let's begin."

Numbers

Set 1: 6 1
Set 2: 2 9 6
Set 3: 6 4 9 6
Set 4: 4 9 1 5 7
Set 5: 7 2 8 1 4 5
Set 6: 1 4 8 5 7 3 6
Set 7: 9 5 6 1 4 2 3 7
Set 8: 2 8 1 7 4 9 3 5 6

You could also use one-syllable words instead of numbers. If you make up your own, make sure the words are not related to one another in any special way.

Words

Set 1: can   me
Set 2: bell big   cap
Set 3: give bank tall rag
Set 4: sit   big   time doll tan
Set 5: ask   net   pet   rag   bug   help
Set 6: pit   red   sat   dog   man   pen   duck
Set 7: wet   see   cat   fan   red   boy   nice go

It's a good idea to stop after your child has trouble stating the digits or words in order. If your child wants to continue, repeat the digits again for him or her. If your child still has difficulty repeating them in order, it's a good idea to engage your child in another activity at this time. Tell your child that you will have him or her try them again at another time.

Story Concentration

This activity is a favorite among children. You can start a story. Then your child must add a sentence to continue the story. You can make it so that the story must make sense or you can have the child help you tell a "silly" story.

Concentration and Following Directions

This is an activity that you and your child can do at any time. Always start with a set of directions that will allow your child to experience success. You can expand or curtail the number of directions you give to your child based on his or her ability to listen and concentrate. Say to your child: "Listen carefully. I will tell you a few things to do. Do not begin until I have finished giving you all the directions and say 'Do it now.' Let's begin."

Clap your hands three times; then put your hands on your knees. Do it now.

Touch your nose; put hands on head. Do it now.

Say "apple" twice; clap hands twice; touch toes twice. Do it now.

Say "happy" three times; turn around three times; hop on your right foot three times. Do it now.

Clap your hands five times; put your hands on your head; say "happy" three times. Do it now.

Raise both hands; stand up and jump up and down four times; say "cheese" four times. Do it now.

Stand up; jump up and down two times; put your hands on your stomach; say "smile" five times. Do it now.

Raise your right hand; put it down. Raise your left hand; put it down. Stand up. Jump up and down three times; say "silly" two times. Do it now.

Stand up; hop on your right leg two times; then hop on your left leg four times. Do it now.

Stand up; jump up and down seven times. Hop on your right leg four times. Do it now.

Jump up and down six times; clap your hands four times; say "I am a good direction follower." Do it now.

86

LISTENING WORD GAMES FOR AGES 4–6

The "If" Word Game

Directions: Listen carefully. I will say something that begins with the word *If*. You have to decide whether you should do what I say or not. Again listen carefully because some of these words may sound silly. Let's try two together. I'll say each one twice.

If the sun is cold, clap your hands three times and say "Hi."

If the sun is cold, clap your hands three times and say "Hi."

ANSWER: Is the sun cold? Of course not. Will you clap your hands three times and say "Hi"? No! Good. Here's another one.

If zebras have stripes, hold up three fingers from one hand and one finger from another.

If zebras have stripes, hold up three fingers from one hand and one finger from another.

ANSWER: Do zebras have stripes? Yes, of course. You should have held up three fingers from one hand and one from the other.

Now, listen carefully. Here we go.

1. If Humpty Dumpty couldn't be put together again, clap your hands three times and tell me what Humpty Dumpty sat on. (You should clap your hands three times and say "wall.")

2. If Jack Sprat could eat no fat, touch your nose with your finger and tell me what his wife could not eat. (You should touch your nose with your finger and say "lean." Jack Sprat could eat no fat and his wife could eat no lean, so between them both they cleaned their platter clean.)

3. If kittens roar and lions meow, hop four times on your right foot. (Do kittens roar and lions meow? No, of course not. It's the other way around. Lions roar and kittens meow. You should do nothing.)

4. If milk comes from a cow, raise your left hand, and say "yes." (You should raise your left hand and say "yes.")

5. If milk can come from a goat, jump up and down three times and say "yes." (You should jump up and down and say "yes.")

6. If a rooster lays eggs, say "cock-a-doodle-doo." (You should say nothing.)

7. If rain is dry, wave good-bye. (You should do nothing.)

8. If the number three comes after the number two, count to ten. (You should count to ten.)

9. If the letter *D* comes after the letter *C,* clap your hands four times. (You should clap your hands four times.)

10. If the number six comes before the number two, jump up and down four times. (You should do nothing.)

11. If the letter *F* comes after the letter *H*, say the alphabet. (You should do nothing.)

12. If a rabbit moves more slowly than a turtle, clap your hands twice. (You should do nothing.)

13. If Little Bo Peep lost her sheep, say "Ba ba" and turn around two times. (You should say "Ba ba" and turn around two times.)

14. If the number ten is bigger than the number five, clap your hands five times and say "yes." (You should clap your hands five times and say "yes.")

15. If the letter *E* comes before the letter *F*, say "yes" and hop three times on your right foot. (You should say "yes" and hop three times on your right foot.)

16. If the number nine is smaller than the number two, say "yes." (You should do nothing.)

17. If *big* is the opposite of *little*, say "yes." (You should say "yes.")

18. If *hot* is the opposite of *cold*, you should clap your hands five times and say "yes." (You should clap your hands five times and say "yes.")

19. If *small* means the same as *little*, you should hop four times on your right foot. (You should hop on your right foot four times and say "yes.")

20. If *begin* is the opposite of *start*, clap your hands nine times. (You should do nothing.)

The Rhyming Word Riddle Game

This game deals with rhyming words—words that sound alike, for example, *fat cat* or *fat rat* or *hot pot* or *big pig*.

I will give you a riddle with lots of clues. You have to answer the riddle. The answer to the riddle is always a rhyming word. Let's do one together.

The word I am thinking of rhymes with *man*.
It also rhymes with *can, tan, ran,* and *fan*.
I use it when I make eggs.
What is it?

Think! What rhymes with *can, tan, ran, fan,* and *man* that you can use to make eggs? Yes, the answer is *pan*. I can make eggs in a pan.

1. The word I am thinking of rhymes with *fat*.
   It also rhymes with *hat, sat, rat,* and *mat*.
   It says "meow."
   What is it? (Answer: cat)

2. The word I am thinking of rhymes with *cat*.
   It also rhymes with *hat, sat,* and *rat*.
   My cat sleeps on it.
   What is it? (Answer: mat)

3. The word I am thinking of rhymes with *fat*.
   It also rhymes with *cat, mat,* and *rat*.
   I wear it on my head.
   What is it? (Answer: hat)

4. The word I am thinking of rhymes with *fat*.
   It also rhymes with *sat, hat,* and *cat*.
   I can hit a ball with it.
   What is it? (Answer: bat)

5. The word I am thinking of rhymes with *get*.
   It also rhymes with *set, met,* and *pet*.
   I get this way when it rains.
   What is it? (Answer: wet)

6. The word I am thinking of rhymes with *set*.
   It also rhymes with *bet, wet,* and *let*.
   I call my kitten this.
   What is it? (Answer: pet)

7. The word I am thinking of rhymes with *far*.
   It also rhymes with *bar* and *tar*.
   I ride in this.
   What is it? (Answer: car)

8. The word I am thinking of rhymes with *car*.
   It also rhymes with *far* and *jar*.
   I can see this at night.
   What is it? (Answer: star)

9. The word I am thinking of rhymes with *fall*.
   It also rhymes with *call* and *mall*.
   I can bounce this.
   What is it? (Answer: ball)

10. The word I am thinking of rhymes with *ball*.
    It also rhymes with *fall* and *mall*.
    I am the opposite of *tall*.
    What is it? (Answer: small)

11. The word I am thinking of rhymes with *win*.
    It also rhymes with *bin* and *tin*.
    I am part of a fish.
    What am I? (Answer: fin)

12. The word I am thinking of rhymes with *fin*.
    It also rhymes with *tin* and *bin*.
    I am part of a face.
    What am I? (Answer: chin)

13. The word I am thinking of rhymes with *chin*.
    It also rhymes with *fin* and *tin*.
    I am the opposite of *lose*.
    What am I? (Answer: win)

14. The word I am thinking of rhymes with *win*.
    It also rhymes with *thin* and *chin*.
    I hold things together.
    What am I? (Answer: pin)

15. The word I am thinking of rhymes with *main*.
    It also rhymes with *chain* and *plain*.
    I come from the sky.
    What am I? (Answer: rain)

16. The word I am thinking of rhymes with *plain*.
    It also rhymes with *main* and *rain*.
    Lots of people ride in me.
    What am I? (Answer: train)

What Am I? Beginning Sound Riddles Game

I will state a riddle. You have to answer it. Let me first give you some examples.

Listen carefully. I am thinking of a bright color that begins like *roll* and *ride*. The answer is *red*. The color red begins like *roll* and *ride*. Also, the words *red, roll,* and *ride* all have the same beginning sound. Let's do another.

Listen carefully. I am thinking of something you play with and can bounce up and down. It begins like *big* and *bike*. The answer is *ball*. You bounce a ball up and down and it begins like *big* and *bike*.

Here's one more. Listen carefully. I am thinking of a pet that barks. It also begins like *dark* and *done*. The answer is *dog*. A dog barks and the word *dog* begins like *dark* and *done*.

1. I am thinking of a number from one to ten that begins like the words *name* and *no*. (Answer: nine)

2. I am thinking of two numbers from one to ten that begin like the words *set* and *so*. (Answer: six, seven)

3. I am thinking of two numbers from one to ten that begin like the words *find* and *fix*. (Answer: four, five)

4. I am thinking of a farm animal that likes to eat a lot and that begins like *pet* and *pan*. (Answer: pig)

5. I am thinking of part of the face that begins like *no* and *name*. (Answer: nose)

6. I am thinking of part of the face that begins like *me* and *mother*. (Answer: mouth)

7. I am thinking of a finger that begins like *thin* and *think*. (Answer: thumb)

8. I am thinking of part of my foot that begins like *too* and *Tom*. (Answer: toes)

9. I am thinking of something you wear on your hand that begins like *red* and *round*. (Answer: ring)

10. I am thinking of something you wear on your head that begins like *hot* and *hand*. (Answer: hat)

11. I am thinking of something that is the opposite of *high* that begins like *leg* and *let*. (Answer: low)

12. I am thinking of something that is the opposite of *old* that begins like *yet* and *you*. (Answer: young)

13. I am thinking of something that is the opposite of *up* that begins like *dark* and *deep*. (Answer: down)

14. I am thinking of something that is the opposite of *stop* that begins like *get* and *gone*. (Answer: go)

15. I am thinking of something that girls wear that begins like *drip* and *dry*. (Answer: dress)

16. I am thinking of something that is part of the body that begins like *stick* and *step*. (Answer: stomach)

17. I am thinking of something that you need to put on an envelope that begins like *stairs* and *stop*. (Answer: stamp)

18. I am thinking of a fruit that begins like *plate* and *plain*. (Answer: plum)

19. I am thinking of an animal that gives milk that begins like *call* and *cake*. (Answer: cow)

20. I am thinking of something you do at night that begins like *slip* and *slipper*. (Answer: sleep)

The Out-of-Place Word Game or The Odd-Word-Out Game

In this game, I will give you some words. You have to listen very carefully because one word in the group does not fit. You have to tell me which word does not belong. Let me give you some examples. Here is the first set of words: *red, green, blue, Kelsey.*

Don't you agree that the words *red, green,* and *blue* go together because they are colors? The word *Kelsey* doesn't belong because it is a name. It isn't a color.

Here is another example: *John, Seth, Melissa, Brian.* All these words are names. However, the name that doesn't belong is *Melissa* because it is the only name that is a girl's name. The other three names are boys' names.

Let's begin. Remember, you must choose the one word that doesn't belong.

dress, coat, cup, hat   (Answer: cup)

kitchen, bedroom, sink, living room   (Answer: sink)

lion, fox, ape, kitten   (Answer: kitten)

dog, horse, cat, tiger   (Answer: tiger)

spoon, knife, fork, pot   (Answer: pot)

chicken, duck, goose, pig   (Answer: pig)

apple, pear, plum, bean   (Answer: bean)

grapes, string beans, beets, potatoes   (Answer: grapes)

roses, tulips, apples, pansies   (Answer: apples)

puppy, kitten, piglet, goose   (Answer: goose)

wet, set, ran, get   (Answer: ran)

cat, sat, bet, mat   (Answer: bet)

fin win, pin, cat   (Answer: cat)

sink, bed, refrigerator, stove   (Answer: bed)

carrot, peach, grape, plum   (Answer: carrot)

bathing suit, scarf, gloves, coat   (bathing suit)

pigeon, canary, fox, robin   (Answer: fox)

main, train, can, rain   (Answer: can)

bake, bite, cake, lake   (Answer: bite)

bike, like, big, hike   (Answer: big)

Epilogue

Looking Backward from 2100: An Ideal School

Let's give play to our imagination and fast forward to the beginning of the 22nd century to view some educational practices and determine if there are any ramifications for today.

To visit a typical school in the year 2100, we need to board a train on a monorail system that surrounds and connects the various communities with one another. In almost no time at all, our train delivers us to the door of a huge spherically-shaped school, known as a learning enhancement center. The school's director, waiting at the door for us, greets us warmly. She says that she hopes we had a good journey and remarks that all children are brought to the school via the cost-effective monorail system.

When we enter the bright school building, we notice two immense skylights in the ceiling and below each is a small space shuttle. The director explains that five schools share these ships, which are used for the students' field trips to other planets. She says that these shuttles connect to space centers that contain large spaceships, which then take students on various space journeys.

We are quite impressed and ask if this is a special school. She states, however, that all schools have similar supplies, equipment, and high curriculum standards. "The state allocates monies equally to all schools. The education funding situation was finally resolved in the second half of the 21st century," she explains.

While walking through the building, we ask the director if there are any children who have difficulty learning in her school. She remarks that almost all schools have such children. She states that they aren't, however, any different from other children, especially intellectually, because most parents involve children in intellectually stimulating experiences from birth onward. "We learned a very long time ago that the children's home background influences how well they do in school," the director comments.

The director then says that we may observe whatever we wish. We answer that we would like to view students and their instructors in action. During our observations, we are struck by the resemblance to some 20th-century educational practices. For example, we note that some pupils are working together in groups, some in pairs, and some individually. We see numerous children interacting with their multi-media sophisticated computers that have huge monitors to accommodate several students. We also see a group of other pupils engaged in an animated manner with a learning enhancement apprentice. The apprentice, an instructor in training, is discussing preparations for the students' field trip to a nearby planet. He wants the students to first access the planet on their computer to have a "virtual reality" experience before the actual visit, so they will know what to expect.

The director explains to us that all teachers in all schools are learning-enhancement master teachers. They are sensitive, perceptive individuals with a keen sense of humor, and well-versed in the knowledge, skills, and strategies they need to be master learning-enhancement experts. She also states that all teachers use a combination of approaches to help their students gain concepts.

"Teachers are very important people in our world. No one is allowed to work with our children unless they have gone through very rigorous training," the director proudly states. The director says further that students absent from school can participate in school activities via their home multi-media interactive computers. And when students return, they meet with an apprentice teacher who helps them acquire any skills or concepts they may have missed. "Early and immediate intervention," she states, "is cost effective. We believe strongly in interweaving instruction with diagnosis and correction. We do not allow any child 'to fall through the cracks.'"

The director emphasizes that parents are important resources and partners in their children's learning. She explains that all parents meet together once every two weeks in the evening via their interactive home computers to discuss what their children are learning. And parents can access their interactive computers at any time to "visit" their children's school environment. "However" the director says, "as important as parents are in their children's learning, it's still the teachers' job to teach the students."

Just then numerous instructors appear and students gather round specific ones. Next, each group goes into a special well-equipped, soundproof room where the teachers present their lessons using direct instructional techniques based on the individual differences of their students.

The bottom line of this imaginative journey into the future is to show that good practices last through the ages. And no matter how advanced a society may become, or how much money is spent, involved parents and master teachers using direct instructional techniques are the keys to good learning.

94